UCHICAGO CCSR
THE UNIVERSITY OF CHICAGO CONSORTIUM ON CHICAGO SCHOOL RESEARCH

RESEARCH BRIEF FEBRUARY 2013

The Use of Technology in Chicago Public Schools 2011
Perspectives from Students, Teachers, and Principals

Stacy B. Ehrlich, Susan E. Sporte, and Penny Bender Sebring

TABLE OF CONTENTS

1 Executive Summary

3 Introduction

Chapter 1
7 Students' Reports of Technology Use

Chapter 2
13 Teachers' Reports of Technology Use and How it Relates to Student Use

Chapter 3
19 Principals' Reports of Technology Use

Chapter 4
25 Interpretive Summary

29 References

31 Appendix

42 Endnotes

Acknowledgements

This report benefited from the efforts and comments of many people who advised and encouraged us to sharpen our analyses and develop a narrative that would be relevant and useful both for the Chicago Public Schools (CPS) and districts across the country. Our colleagues at the University of Chicago Consortium on Chicago School Research (CCSR) were instrumental in providing feedback and inspiration. We thank Bronwyn McDaniel, Elaine Allensworth, Holly Hart, René Crespin, and Emily Krone for their thoughtful and thorough comments on versions of this paper; Stuart Luppescu for assisting in the creation of our survey measures; and Eric Brown and Kate Julian for ongoing feedback as we conducted this work. We are particularly indebted to James Sebastian, who provided a great amount of technical support and guidance as we conducted our analyses.

We also appreciate our Steering Committee for engaging in discussion and providing insights on this topic. Two members, Veronica Anderson and Stacy Norris, gave us specific input and suggestions. We learned a great deal from conversations with several Chicago Public Schools (CPS) staff members. In particular, John Connolly and John Mellios provided encouragement and on-the-ground context for the questions we were asking in this report. Without the broader support from CPS, we would not have been able to conduct the surveys and collect the data on which this report is based.

Lastly, we would like to thank Connie Yowell and An-Me Chung at the John D. and Catherine T. MacArthur Foundation for their continuous and generous support of CCSR and, in particular, for pushing us to think in new directions about the relevance and necessity of research on digital media.

This report was produced by UChicago CCSR's publications and communications staff: Emily Krone, Director for Outreach and Communication; Bronwyn McDaniel, Communications and Research Manager; and Jessica Puller, Communications Specialist.

Graphic Design: Jeff Hall Design
Photography: Jeff Hall, Cynthia Howe, and David Schalliol
Editing: Ann Lindner

2.2013/pdf/jh.design@rcn.com

THE USE OF TECHNOLOGY IN CHICAGO PUBLIC SCHOOLS

Executive Summary

Technology use is ubiquitous in America's colleges and most workplaces, and it is fast becoming accepted as fact that all students—elementary and high school—must be exposed to technology. Whether schools are doing this is an open question.

A 2002 report by the University of Chicago Consortium on Chicago School Research (CCSR) revealed large differences in how well schools in Chicago were structured to support student and teacher use of technology. Since then, technology use has become an integral part of people's work and private lives. This report attempts to update previous CCSR research on technology use in Chicago Public Schools (CPS) by focusing on the most basic skills and experiences students need in order to become technologically literate—e.g., the extent to which students are using technology for school and whether factors such as school culture and expectations of technology use by their teachers and principals contribute to this.

KEY FINDINGS IN THIS REPORT INCLUDE:

The vast majority of CPS students have access to the internet at home, but many use technology infrequently in school.

- Ninety-two percent of students in grades six through 12 report having access to the internet at home.
- Only about half of these students use technology at least weekly for school, and 20 to 30 percent never use it or use it rarely—at most once or twice a semester.

The extent to which students report using technology varies considerably. Some of this variability has to do with each student's individual characteristics and experiences, but some of it also has to do with the school they attend.

- Students use technology for school in varying amounts, but student background characteristics —including gender, special education status, socio-economic status, and achievement—explain only a small amount of the difference in students' use of technology.
- Students in schools with higher-achieving students use computers and the internet more than other students, as do those who attend selective enrollment high schools.

There is also considerable variation across schools in how much teachers use technology and how much support teachers feel for the use of technology. Moreover, students who use technology more frequently attend schools where teachers also use technology more and expect more frequent use by their students.

- Across all school types, elementary and high school teachers (70 percent) use the internet for lesson preparation regularly (at least weekly), while only 45 to 50 percent use computer programs in delivering lessons at least weekly. Furthermore, only 45 to 50 percent ask their students to complete course work using technology on a weekly basis. However, most teachers (70 percent) believe that their school has a culture encouraging the use of technology for instruction and communication.

- Teacher use and school technology culture vary by school type. Teachers in magnet elementary and selective enrollment high schools use technology more, expect their students to use technology more, and feel a more supportive culture for the use of technology in their schools.

- The variation in student and teacher use across schools is related. Students tend to use technology more in schools where teachers also use technology more. Teachers in these schools report a more supportive culture for integrating technology into their teaching, and believe that their school is doing a better job preparing students to be technologically literate than other schools.

School leaders play a role in setting expectations and providing supports for technology use.

- More than 60 percent of principals say they set high expectations for their teachers to integrate technology into their classrooms, but far fewer believe that their teachers are using technology to help students interact more with each other.

- Roughly half of all principals feel that their students are being prepared to be technologically literate; an additional 40 percent "somewhat" agree with this statement.

- Students and teachers use technology more, and feel more support for integrating technology into teaching and learning, in schools where principals say they have higher expectations for use.

- Teachers also use technology more, and feel more support for the use of technology, in schools where principals report fewer barriers to the use of computers and technology.

This report highlights the unequal use of technology across schools in Chicago. Some schools have students, teachers, and principals who use technology regularly as part of their communication, teaching, and learning, while others have students and staff who barely use computers at all. *This inequality deserves attention.* Schools can provide high quality technology support, equalizing the experience of all students. While students and teachers bring their own external experiences to the school, the support within the building can be quite powerful. Indeed, findings from this report suggest that increasing teacher and principal use and expectations for technology use are viable methods for increasing student engagement with computers and the internet. Given the growing importance of technology literacy for functioning in any kind of job—as well as for communicating, obtaining information and critiquing its veracity, and creating new products—there is a critical need to encourage technology integration into teaching and learning for all students.

Introduction

Technological literacy is becoming an essential skill for students to learn, and teaching this can be a challenging task for districts. In light of this shifting landscape, we assess technology use in Chicago Public Schools by examining survey data on student, teacher, and principal perceptions of technology use and culture within their schools.

Technology use is ubiquitous in America's colleges and most workplaces, and it is fast becoming accepted as fact that all students—in both elementary and high schools—must be exposed to technology. This exposure is intended to develop the technological literacy that will prepare them for a future that promises to be evermore dominated by the use of digital technologies and platforms. The growing recognition of the need for technological literacy can be seen in new national standards and assessments. For example, the National Assessment of Educational Progress began pilot testing of an assessment of technological literacy to fourth-, eighth-, and twelfth-graders in 2012, with full administration beginning in 2014. In addition, the new Common Core State Standards (CCSS) highlight the need to incorporate technology and the internet into all aspects of education for students. Students who meet the new standards are described as:

> ...those who employ technology thoughtfully to enhance their reading, writing, speaking, listening, and language use. They tailor their searches online to acquire useful information efficiently, and they integrate what they learn using technology with what they learn offline. They are familiar with the strengths and limitations of various technological tools and mediums and can select and use those best suited to their communication goals.[1]

Technology is also embedded throughout a range of mathematics standards, which call for all students to understand when and in what ways technology can aid in the understanding and execution of mathematics ideas and concepts.

While technological literacy is increasingly viewed as critical, recent evidence indicates that 43 percent of students nationally do not leave high school feeling prepared to use technology in college or the workplace.[2] Low-income students are the least likely to use the internet and other technologies in ways that prepare them for college.[3] Furthermore, low-income students are least likely to be exposed to technology at home—due to lack either of equipment or of others with enough knowledge to teach them how to utilize these resources.[4]

Many researchers and decision-makers are focused on understanding the ways in which teachers integrate technology into their classrooms to support student learning; however, before we can focus on the higher-level goals, there is a need to establish whether technology available in the schools is being utilized. While there is no clear picture of student, teacher, and principal use of technology across the country, we can examine this for the Chicago Public Schools (CPS), the country's third largest school system. The University of Chicago Consortium on Chicago School Research's (CCSR) rich database of CPS survey data collected over the last 20 years provides an excellent opportunity to study trends in technology use over time in a large, urban district serving primarily low-income students.

Previous CCSR research from a decade ago showed that the lack of hardware, software, and technological knowledge among educators in CPS was a key barrier to the integration of technology into schools.[5] By 2005, some of those issues —such as networking and computer supply issues—had been addressed; however, students were still using computers "infrequently," teachers still reported little professional development around integrating technology into their course work, and teachers were not incorporating technology assignments into students' everyday work.[6] While we do not know if CPS' historic and current patterns of technology use differ from other districts across the country, we do know that CPS serves over 400,000 urban students each year; as such, it is important to take stock of where the district is now and how far it needs to go.

Today, 10 years after CCSR's first technology report was released, technology use has become an integral part of people's work and private lives. Not only are computers ubiquitous, but smart phones, tablets, and other devices have expanded technology's reach for most adults and an increasing number of teens. The increased focus on technology in schools is also energized by the hope that with better integration, students will become more engaged, participating in deeper learning supported by individualized instruction. We begin here by looking at the most basic skills and experiences students need in order to become technologically literate—how frequently are students using technology for school, and do their learning environments contribute to this? We find that while some students are using technology at least once a week for school-related work, 40 percent or more do not. Students in higher-achieving schools use technology more, but there are other factors at the school level that are related to student use. Thus, we also ask whether students are being taught by teachers and principals who value the use of technology in education, whether they are surrounded by teachers who exhibit how to use these tools, and whether barriers exist to use in the school. And in fact, these do matter. How much teachers and principals expect technology to be used for school and how frequently teachers themselves use computers help explain differences in how much students use technology.

These questions set the stage, helping us better understand the extent to which computers and the internet are currently used on a basic level by CPS students, and the extent to which teachers and principals set the expectations for use. Only once we know this can we begin to understand the best ways to integration of technology into learning and teaching.

Methods

Data
Data reported in this paper come from three sources: administrative data from Chicago Public Schools (CPS); survey data collected in spring 2011 from students, teachers, and principals; and student survey data collected in spring 2012. The survey administrations were conducted by CCSR.

Administrative Data
Administrative data on students and schools used in this paper are collected by the Chicago Public Schools and shared with CCSR. Student background data are shared with CCSR twice a year (September and May) on all students in the system.

Survey Data
The My Voice, My School survey is co-sponsored by CCSR and Chicago Public Schools. The survey is used as a school improvement tool as well as a research tool.

In 2011, students, teachers, and principals were surveyed. Seventy-four percent of students (146,571), 49 percent of teachers (11,806), and 61 percent of principals (411) filled out the survey. On each survey, there was a set of technology-related questions. All survey data were collected online using school computer labs. School staff facilitated data collection and monitored response rates.

In 2012, CCSR again surveyed students and teachers across the district. Unlike the 2011 survey, the 2012 survey only asked technology-related questions of students, not teachers. There was a student response rate of 74 percent (143,816).

Because in 2011 the survey was administered online for the first time, and because we are focusing on technology-related questions, we examined whether there was bias in teachers' responses to our survey questions. In particular, we were concerned that response rates might be lower in schools with less use of technology and that this might bias the averages. For example, if teacher use is significantly related to student use and if there is bias, we might expect that teachers in schools where students use technology less would be less likely to complete our survey. However, we find no indication of teacher response bias. Teacher response rates are similar in schools where students are least likely to use technology and in schools where students report some of the highest uses of technology (elementary schools: 64.5 percent versus 66.8 percent response rates; high schools: 51.1 percent versus 53.6 percent teacher response rates).

To see more details about data collection and survey data quality, go to **http://ccsr.uchicago.edu/surveys/documentation**

Analyses
We present findings in two ways throughout this report:

1. The graphs and overall percentages of responses to survey items are based on descriptive analyses of how students, teachers, and principals responded to specific survey questions that were asked of them.

2. Using responses to individual survey questions, we also created "measures" or "scales." These are groups of questions that share the same underlying concept. Using Rasch analysis, we assign scores to individuals based on their answers to a set of questions. **See Appendix B** for a description of how we created measures included in this report. We then use characteristics of individuals and schools in Hierarchical Linear Models (HLM) to explain some of the differences in individuals' measure scores.[7] These multi-level analyses help to account for the clustering of students or teachers within schools, where they share similar environments. For example, we can determine how much of the difference in technology use between students is due to their own individual characteristics versus the schools they attend. In addition, using such statistical models allows us to determine whether the patterns noted in the descriptive analyses remain when we simultaneously take multiple variables into account. (**See Appendix B** for more details on our HLM models.)

CHAPTER 1

Students' Reports of Technology Use

Key Findings

- **Almost 92 percent of students** in grades six through 12 have some type of access to the internet at home, with 75 percent saying they connect to the internet using a high-speed connection.

- **Despite high levels of access at home**, only about half of CPS students use technology at least weekly for school, and 20 to 30 percent never use it or use it rarely—at most once or twice a semester.

- **Student background characteristics** explain only a small amount of the difference in students' use of technology:

- Male students and high-risk students (students receiving special education services, low socio-economic students, and students who are old for their grade) use technology less than other students.

- Secondary school students with higher ninth-grade achievement scores use technology more than those with lower achievement scores.

- **The school that a student attends** explains some of the differences in students' use of technology.

- Students in elementary and high schools with higher achievement levels use technology more than students in other elementary and high schools.

- Even after taking into account the achievement of students in the school, students in selective enrollment high schools use technology more than other high school students.

- **After taking these characteristics into account**, we still find that much of the difference in student technology use is unexplained.

We begin by examining how often students interact with computers in schools for what we would consider some of the more basic uses—for example, using the internet for research, or using common computer programs, like Excel or PowerPoint, to complete their school work. While we do not suggest that such basic uses are sufficient to prepare students to be technologically proficient, we do believe they are a necessary baseline. Therefore, we first explore the extent to which students in the Chicago Public Schools are using computers in these fundamental ways.

Where Students Stand: Digital Access and Preferences for Learning and Using Technology

If we are to have any expectations that students use computers and technology for school, we need to first establish that these students have access to technology, the internet, and people who can provide help with these tools. While the technology divide has historically centered around access to computers and the internet, more recently it has been shifting to something more than just physical access. The "access divide" is now about differences in the access to knowledge of how to effectively use technologies.[8] Particularly in urban settings, access to technology and the internet has been increasing for young adults.[9] We find this to be true for students in CPS as well. According to our 2012 survey (**see Table A.1 in Appendix A** for 2012 student survey items on technology), almost 92 percent of students in grades six through 12 have some kind of access to the internet at home, with 75 percent saying they connect to the internet using a high-speed connection. While there are slight differences between students of different backgrounds, over 90 percent of students in each racial/ethnic group and poverty level report having internet access, and between 70 and 83 percent of students have access to high-speed internet.[10] In addition, almost 90 percent of all students say they have someone both in and outside of school to go to if they need help using the computer to complete a school project. Therefore, as of 2012, most students in CPS—regardless of their neighborhood, background characteristics, or whether they are at the middle or high school grade level—*do* have access to the internet and do have people to turn to when they need help with computers.

Students also *prefer* to use technology to access information. Based on responses to the 2012 survey (see Figure 1), most students prefer to find information online rather than offline; only 10 percent of students prefer searching for information offline. In addition, 40 percent of students say they remember information better when they read something on a screen. Another 42 percent took a neutral stance between on-screen and off-screen reading. These figures indicate that for more than 80 percent of students, using a computer, iPad, or tablet to read information would not be worse than— and could perhaps be better than—reading information from a textbook.

FIGURE 1

Student preferences for finding information and reading materials

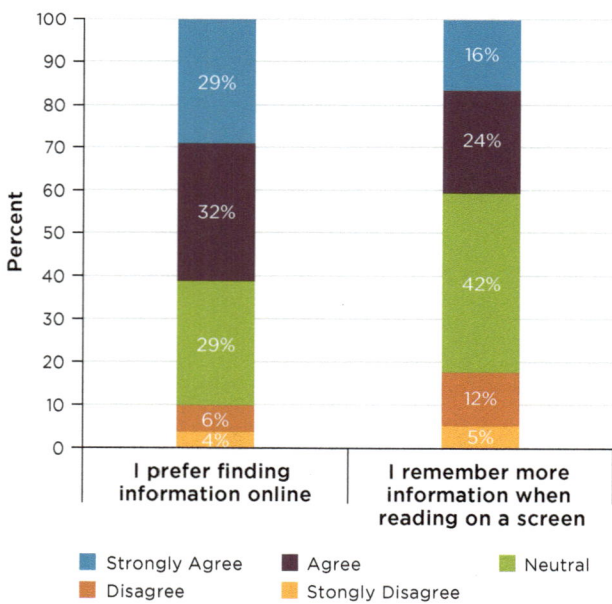

Note: Ns = 119,437 and 118,812, respectively.

The high level of access that students have to the internet and their preferences for searching for information online would seem to present an opportunity for schools. With this in mind, we examine what technology use for and in school looks like.

To What Extent are Students Using Technology for School?

At least half of all CPS students in grades six through 12 use the internet and computer programs for school-related work at least once each week. But this means that the other half of students use these tools less frequently. In addition, most students—70 percent of them—do not use technology regularly to create something new and creative for schools. This overall low level of use is concerning given that supporters of technology integration believe that for integration to have an effect on learning, students need to be engaged with technology at least once a week.[11]

Figure 2 shows the responses of students in the middle grades and high school years to three questions on our survey: how often they (1) use the internet to find information for school assignments; (2) use computer programs (e.g., Excel or PowerPoint[12]) to complete school work; and (3) use technology to make something new and creative (e.g., blog, video, website) for a class or other school-based program (see Table A.2 for full survey items). The use of the internet for research purposes and the use of common computer programs touch on the basic ways in which technology is used in all kinds of settings once students graduate. The third type of use centers on whether students are being given opportunities to use technology in new and creative ways and in ways that allow them to express themselves in various formats, encouraging a more student-centered mode of learning.[13]

While the use of technology for school is not a daily, or even weekly, activity for many students, this is an improvement over rates reported by CPS students in 2005, when just over 40 percent of students used the internet weekly and less than 20 percent used computer programs at least weekly (see Figure 3). In fact, in 2005, almost 30 percent of students said they were never required to use computer programs for school work.[14]

FIGURE 2
While roughly half of CPS students use technology at least weekly for school, 20 to 30 percent rarely or never do

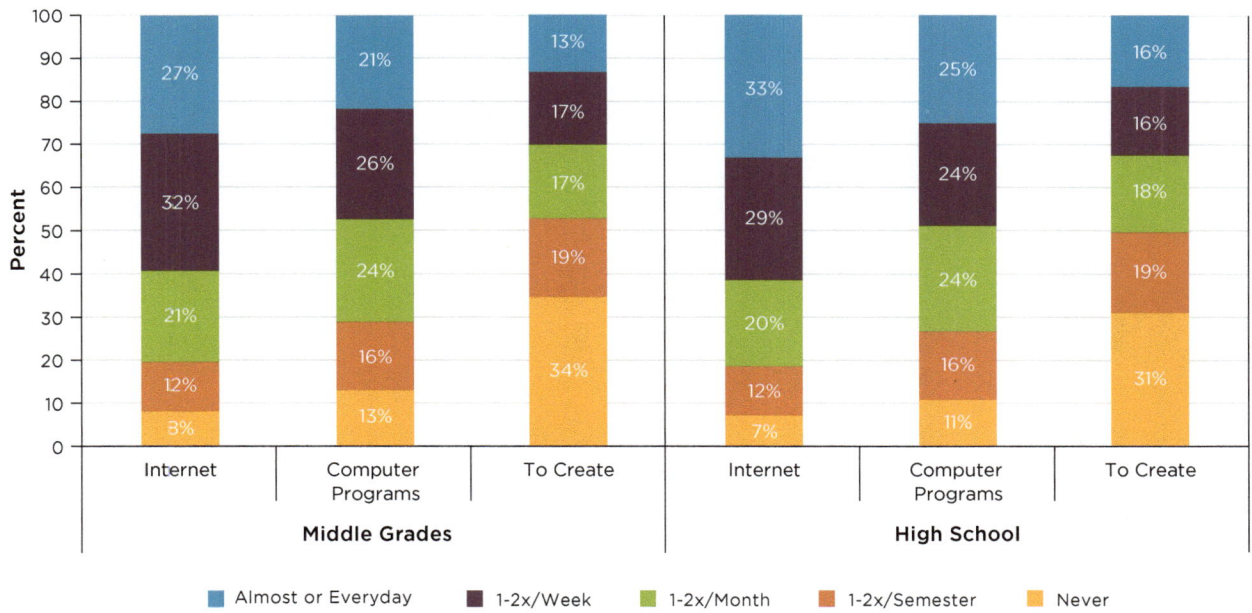

Note: At the elementary level, only students in grades six through eight (the middle grades) were administered the survey. At the elementary level, Ns were between 59,942 and 60,207. At the high school level, Ns were between 63,333 and 63,450.

FIGURE 3
Students' internet and computer program usage for school has increased since 2005

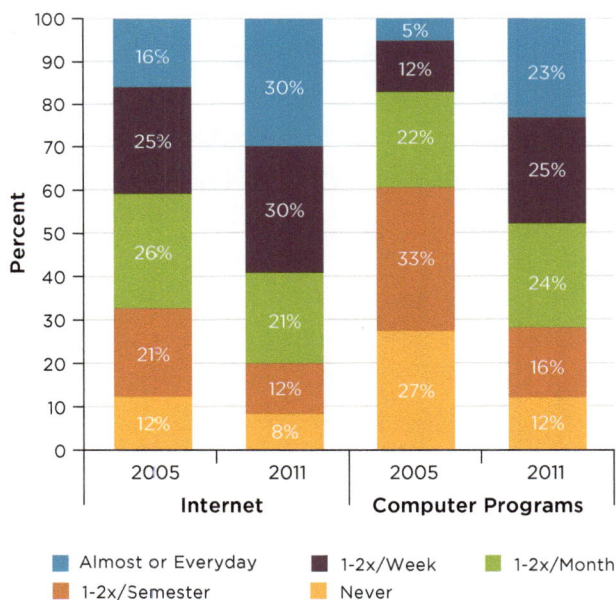

Note: Ns in 2005 are between 103,796 and 105,495. Ns in 2011 are between 123,275 and 123,611. 2005 Computer Programs use was calculated as the average response category for two items: using Excel and using PowerPoint (see Table A.3 for full survey items).

While **Figure 2** paints an overall picture of technology use, there is considerable variation depending on students' background characteristics and what type of school they attend. We now explore where these differences exist.

How Technology Use Varies Across Students

Technology use varies—but only modestly—among students with different background characteristics (**Figure 4**). We display findings for high school students, but the patterns are similar, albeit slightly muted, for middle-grade students. In addition, we focus on one particular question—how frequently students use the internet to find information for school assignments—but the findings are similar for the use of computer programs.[15]

These findings include:

- Males say they use the internet to look up information for school assignments less often than females do. Fifty-six percent of high school males use the internet at least one to two times a week to look up information for school, while 65 percent of females say they do.

FIGURE 4

There are small differences in how often students use the internet for school assignments based on background characteristics

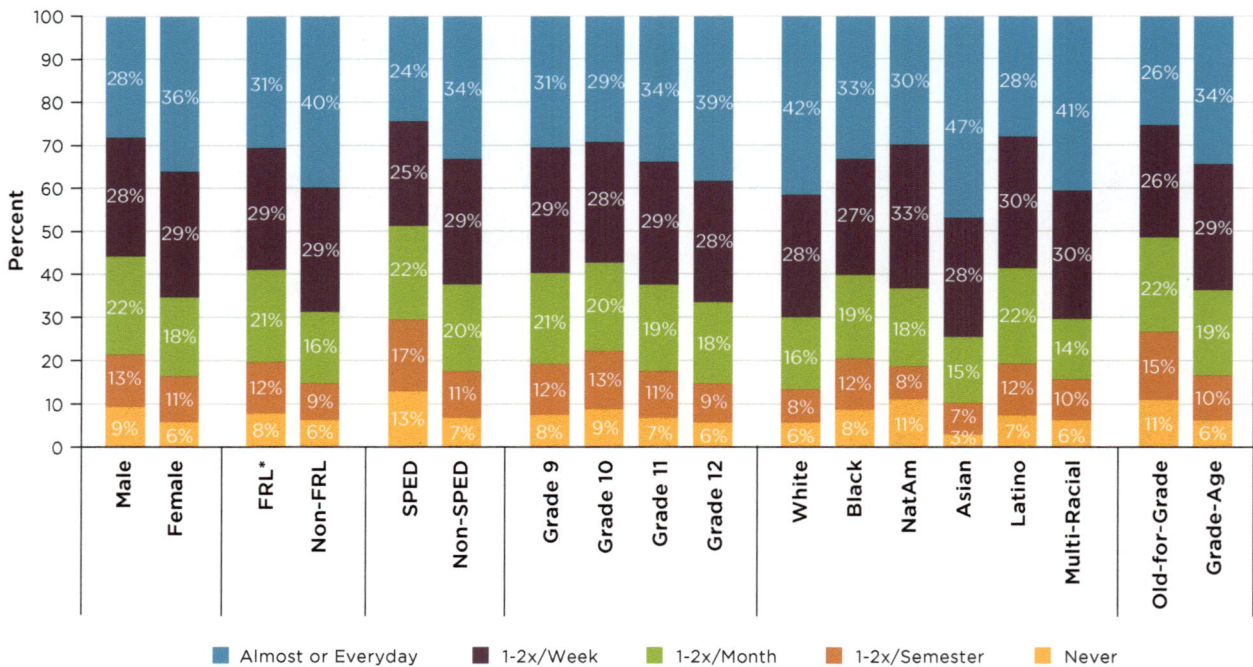

Note: * FRL = Eligible to receive free or reduced-price lunch. N = 63,433.

- Overall, high-risk students do not use the internet for school as much as other students do. This includes students receiving special education services, students who receive free or reduced-price lunch, and students who are old for their grade.
- White, Asian, and multi-racial students report using the internet for school more than African American, Native American, and Latino students do.
- For high school students, how often they use the internet for school seems to be related to grade level. Tenth-grade students report the least internet usage, while twelfth-grade students report the most.
- As shown in **Figure 5**, high school students who score in the top quartile on the EXPLORE test upon entry into high school are almost twice as likely to use the internet every day or almost every day compared to high school students who score in the bottom quartile on the EXPLORE test.[16]

Hierarchical linear models (**see Methods on p.8 and Appendix B** for descriptions of our models) allow us to decipher which of students' individual characteristics may be driving the differences in overall "Student Technology Use."[17] For example, we might wonder whether the less frequent use of technology by African American students holds true when we also take into account effects for income. We find that most of the ndividual differences seen in **Figure 4** remain, but others—such as some of the racial differences—do not (**see Tables C.1 and C.2 in Appendix C, Model A**). Males, Latinos, and at-risk students report using technology less than other students—differences that are small but statistically significant. And, consistent with **Figure 5**, students with higher achievement, at both the elementary and high school levels, are more likely to use technology more frequently. It is worth noting that, although differences continue to exist for some racial groups, the difference between African American and white high school students fade when taking into account all factors at the same time; they are explained by other differences, such as the school these students attend.[18]

How Technology Use Differs Across Schools

While some of the difference in the extent to which students use computers for school comes from the individual characteristics and experiences of those

FIGURE 5

High school students with higher EXPLORE scores report using the internet for school more frequently

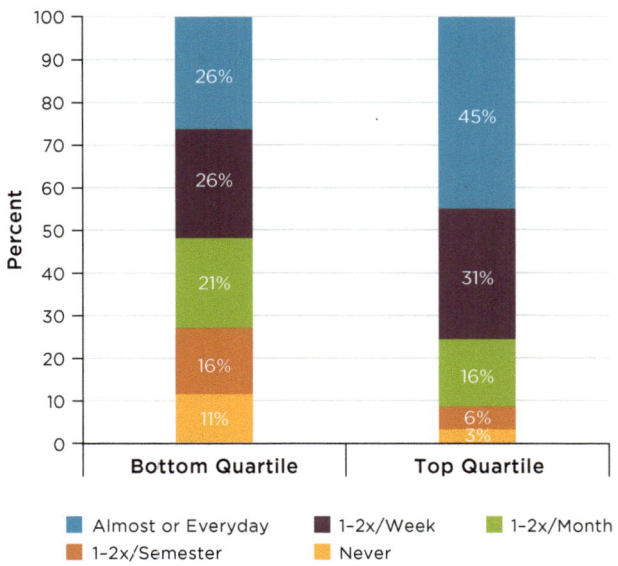

Note: Total N=62,228. Bottom quartile N = 14,302; Top quartile N= 15,066 Quartiles based on full population of EXPLORE takers in 2010.

students, difference in use can also be explained by which schools those students attend. Indeed, the proportion of students in a particular school who say they use the internet frequently (at least weekly) ranges from 12 percent in one school to 89 percent in another school.

One school-level factor that explains these variations in technology use at the high school level is the type of school—neighborhood, selective enrollment, or charter. From the descriptives displayed in **Figure 6**, we see that students in selective enrollment schools are almost twice as likely to use the internet almost every day or every day compared with high school students in neighborhood and charter schools. More than 80 percent of students in selective enrollment high schools use the internet weekly for school, compared with 57 to 62 percent of students in neighborhood and charter schools. In addition to having fewer students use computers on a weekly basis, roughly 20 percent of students in neighborhood and charter schools either report never using the internet, or using it only one to two times per semester.

These differences in student technology use by school type are consistent with our model results. Among middle-grade students, those who attend a school with higher achievement levels use technology more often (**Table C.1, Model B in Appendix C**). Among high school students, those who go to a school with higher average achievement, and those who attend a selective enrollment high school, use technology more often, regardless of the individual characteristics of that student (**Table C.2, Model B in Appendix C**). Controlling for student-level characteristics, high school students attending a charter school also use technology more frequently than students in neighborhood schools.

Differences in Technology Use Cannot Be Fully Explained by Student Background or School Type

As is generally the case in education research, the differences that we measure between students at the same school are larger than the differences from one school to another. That is, student background characteristics tend to trump school characteristics. Yet, in this case, the background characteristics that often explain differences in school performance do not fully explain why students use technology more or less frequently. Very little of the student-level variation could be explained by their gender, race, test scores, or social status. Thus, there are likely other things—things we did not measure—impacting how much students use technology for school, such as varied interests in technology.

Similarly, our school-level variables (school type, average achievement of students, and average socioeconomic status of the students in that school) do not explain all of the school-by-school differences in technology use. As noted previously, students who attend schools with other high achievers and those who attend selective enrollment schools use technology for school —including the internet, computer programs, and to create new products—more often than those in schools with lower-achieving students and those who attend either neighborhood or charter schools. However, there are differences that remain unexplained, suggesting there are other factors related to student technology use besides those included in our models. To better understand those factors, we next explore how teachers use technology and whether there is a supportive culture around technology use in these schools.

FIGURE 6

Students in selective enrollment high schools use the internet for school-related work more frequently than students in other types of schools

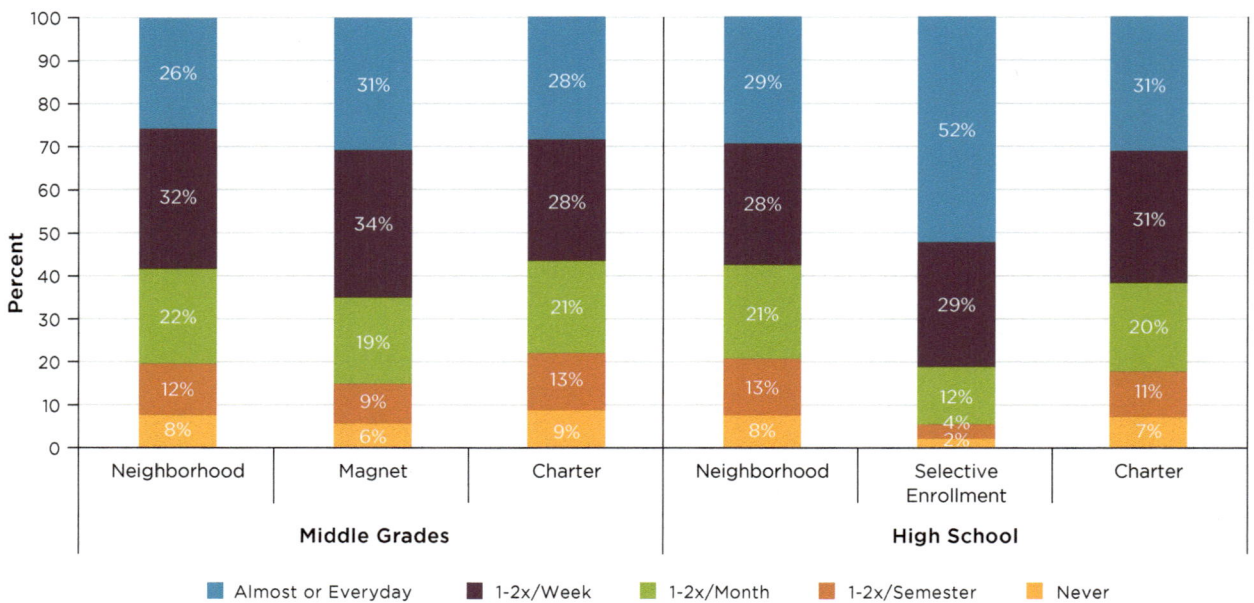

Note: Elementary (N = 58,278); High School (N = 61,629)

CHAPTER 2

Teachers' Reports of Technology Use and How It Relates to Student Use

Key Findings

- **Most elementary and high school teachers (70 percent) use the internet for lesson preparation regularly** (at least weekly), while only 45 to 50 percent use computer programs in delivering lessons at least weekly. Furthermore, only 45 to 50 percent ask their students to complete course work using technology on a weekly basis.

- **Most teachers (more than 70 percent) also agree that their school has a culture encouraging the use of technology for instruction and communication.**

- **Teacher use and school culture vary by school type.** Teachers in magnet elementary and selective enrollment high schools use technology more, expect their students to use technology more, and feel a more supportive culture for the use of technology in their schools.

- **Teacher reports of their own technology use and of their school culture are related to how frequently students in those schools use technology.** These teacher reports help explain some of the school-by-school differences seen in student use.

Student use of technology does not exist in a vacuum. In the last chapter, we saw great variation in student technology use based on whether they attend a selective enrollment school or one with other high-achieving students. If the goal is to make computer and internet usage a regular occurrence in all schools and for all students—and not just the 6 percent who attend selective enrollment schools—what can we learn about the expectations and supports that teachers provide? One would expect that greater school-wide use, higher expectations by teachers, and a more supportive culture for technology use might affect how often students use technology. We explore this possibility in this chapter.

We first examine how frequently teachers report using technology in various ways, the extent to which teachers across CPS feel support for technology use, and how much they believe their schools are preparing students to be technologically literate. We then explore whether variation by school type mirrors that found with student use. Finally, we consider whether teacher use and school culture are related to student use of technology and can help explain some of the variations in student use that remained at the end of our last chapter.

Teachers' Use of Technology and School Culture

How Frequently Do Teachers Use Technology in Their Instruction?

The majority of teachers—about 70 percent—say they use the internet at least once a week to help with lesson planning (**Figure 7; see Table A.4 in Appendix A for survey items**). However, a smaller proportion of teachers—fewer than half—report using technology while they are teaching. Furthermore, less than half report that they expect their students to use technology for their school work on a weekly basis. This aligns with how often students report using technology for school work, suggesting that unless teachers expect their students to use technology to support their learning, students do not incorporate computers and technology into the work they do for school.[19] As **Figure 7** shows, there are no appreciable differences between elementary school and high school teachers.

FIGURE 7

Most teachers use the internet weekly for preparation, but fewer expect their students to regularly use technology for course work

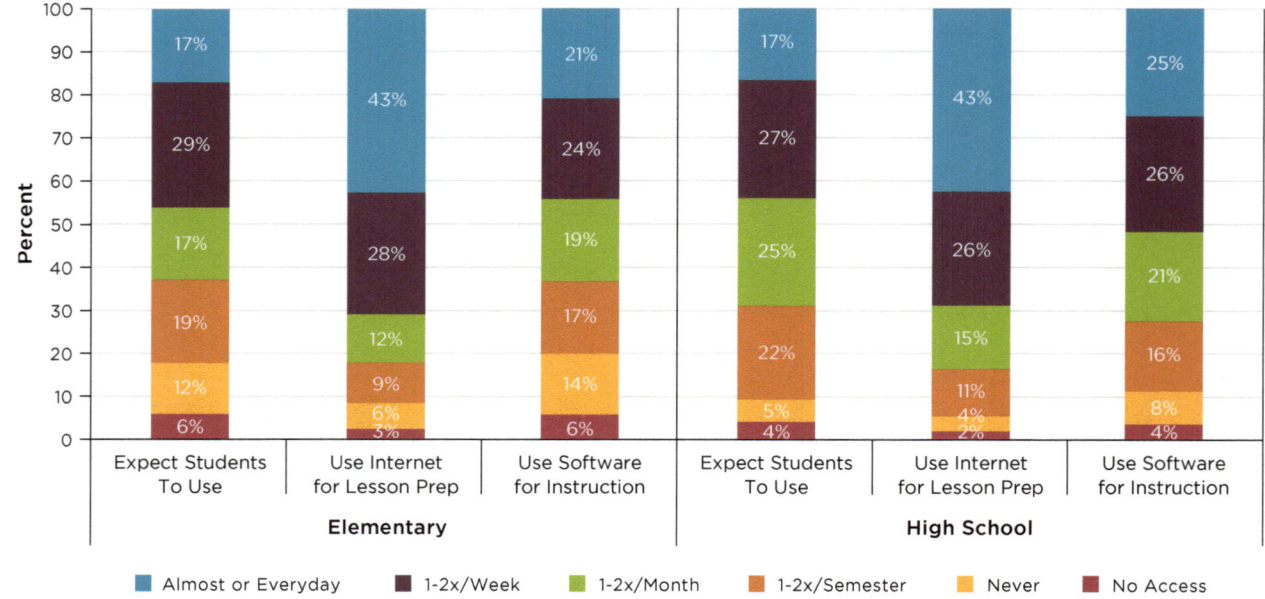

Note: Elementary (Ns were between 7,073 and 7,105); High School (Ns were between 3,115 and 3,128)

To What Extent Do Schools Have a Culture that Supports the Use of Technology?

Teachers are somewhat positive about the extent to which their school culture supports the use of technology. At least 70 percent of CPS teachers report that they "somewhat" or "very much" agree that their school culture encourages the use of technology for instruction and communication (**Figure 8**). Most also feel that their school is preparing students to be technologically proficient (**"Preparing students" in Figure 8**). However, almost one-third of teachers report low levels of support for technology use. These differences varied both within schools, and across school types.

Differences Across School Types

In Chapter 2, we learned that there are differences in how frequently students use technology based on the type of school they attend. The same is true for teachers. Both teacher use and their reports of how supportive their school culture is of technology use differ by school type, particularly at the high school level. Teachers in selective enrollment schools use computers and the internet more frequently than their counterparts in charter and neighborhood schools, and they are more likely to feel a supportive culture around the use of technology in their school.

Teacher Technology Use

To explore varying levels of teacher technology use across school types, we look at one specific item—how often teachers expect their students to use technology in completing their class work or assignments.[20] Schools differ significantly in teacher expectations for use: in some schools, none of the teachers expects weekly computer use by students, while in other schools, 100 percent of teachers do. This is a notable difference; some students attend schools where teachers have very low expectations of computer use, while others are exposed to regular use across many of their classes. These differences in levels of expectation for student use differ by school type, especially at the high school level. Nearly 65 percent of teachers in selective enrollment high schools have weekly technology-use expectations for their students, while just over 30 percent of teachers in charter schools and 40 percent of teachers in neighborhood schools do (**Figure 9**). Statistical modeling using "Teacher Use" (a combined measure of teacher use and expectation for student use) confirmed

FIGURE 8

Most teachers feel that their school culture encourages the use of technology

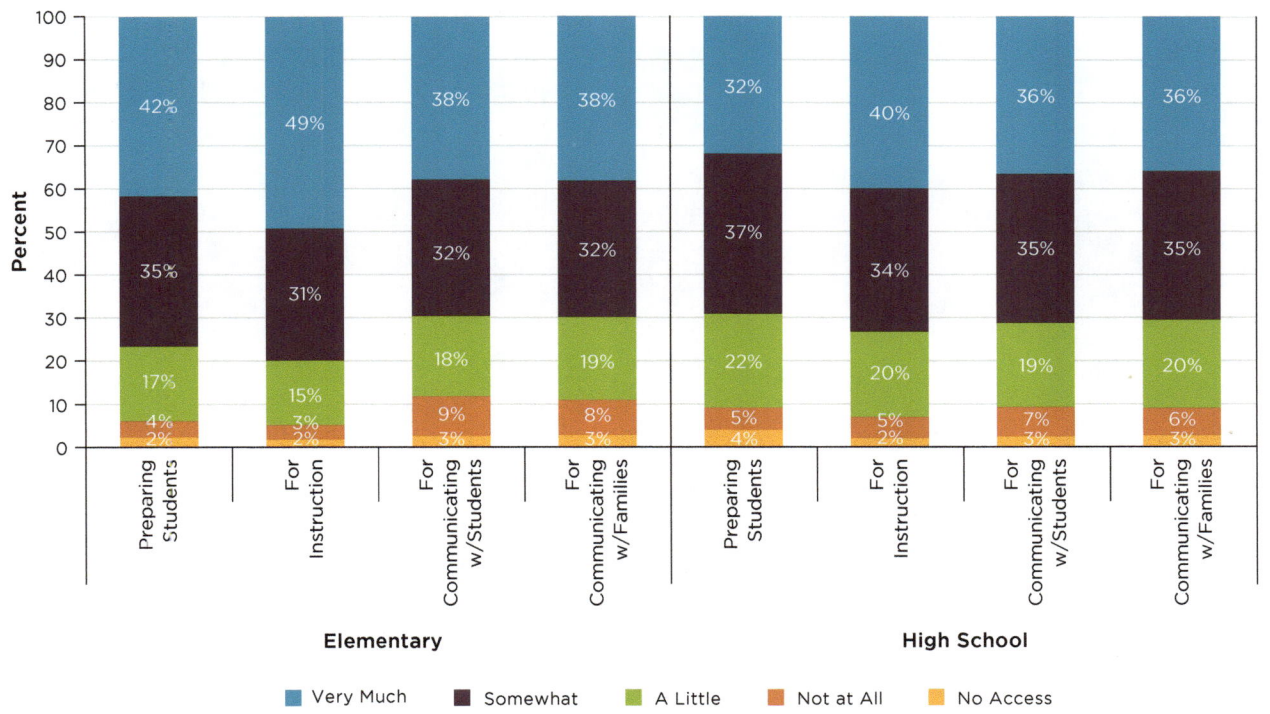

Note: Elementary (Ns were between 7,146 and 7,213); High School (Ns were between 3,118 and 3,149)

FIGURE 9

A greater proportion of teachers in magnet/selective enrollment schools have expectations for frequent student use, while a smaller proportion of teachers in charter schools do

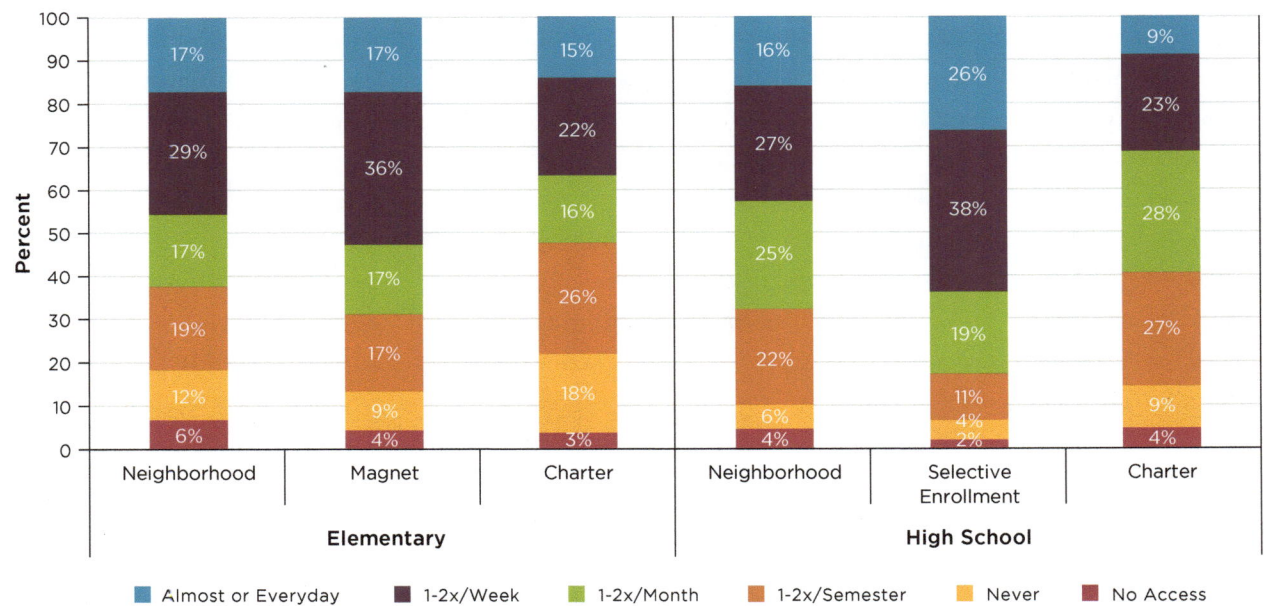

Note: Elementary (N = 6,777); High School (N = 3,145)

FIGURE 10

Teachers' beliefs that schools are preparing students to be technologically proficient are highest in selective enrollment schools and lowest in charter schools

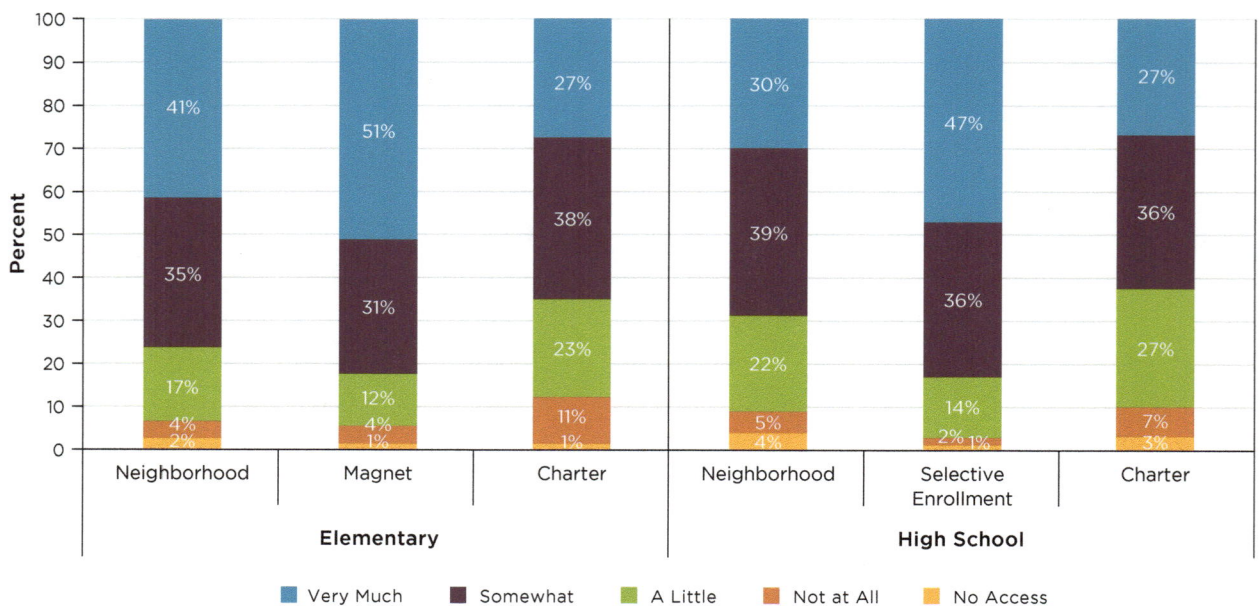

Note: Elementary (N = 6,871); High School (N = 3,168).

the patterns revealed in the descriptive statistics. At the high school level, even after taking into account background characteristics of students, teachers in selective enrollment schools had the highest expectations for technology use. Teachers in charter schools had expectations and use that was similar to those in neighborhood schools (**see Table C.3 in Appendix C**). In addition, the most consistent variable related to teacher use and expectations for both elementary and high school teachers was school-level achievement (ISAT reading scores in elementary schools, and incoming EXPLORE scores in high schools): teachers in schools with higher achievement scores and those in selective enrollment high schools report using computers and expecting their students to use computers more frequently.

Teacher-Reported School Culture for Technology Use

Similarly, there are wide differences in reports of school culture across schools. Again, there are some schools where many teachers report feeling a supportive culture for the use of technology, while in others virtually none do. To understand these variations, we look at one specific question: how much teachers believe that their school is preparing students to be technologically proficient.[21] Teachers in magnet elementary and selective enrollment high schools are more likely to "very much" agree—at around 50 percent—that their school is preparing students to be technologically proficient (**Figure 10**), and over 80 percent agree at least "somewhat." To compare, only 30 percent of teachers in neighborhood high schools and 27 percent in charter schools agree.

Our multi-level models confirmed most of these findings, although the differences between charter and neighborhood schools were eliminated. Our models did continue to find that teachers in schools with higher average student achievement are more likely to agree that there is a supportive school culture for the use and integration of technology into teaching (**see Table C.4 in Appendix C**). Therefore, not only do higher-achieving students report using technology more for school, but the teachers in those higher-performing schools are the ones who are most likely to exhibit similar behavior, require that their students integrate computers into their research and other school work, and feel more encouragement for the use of technology. While there is a clear association, we cannot be sure whether this

FIGURE 11

Students in magnet/selective enrollment schools are more likely to have teachers talk about assessing reliability of information found online

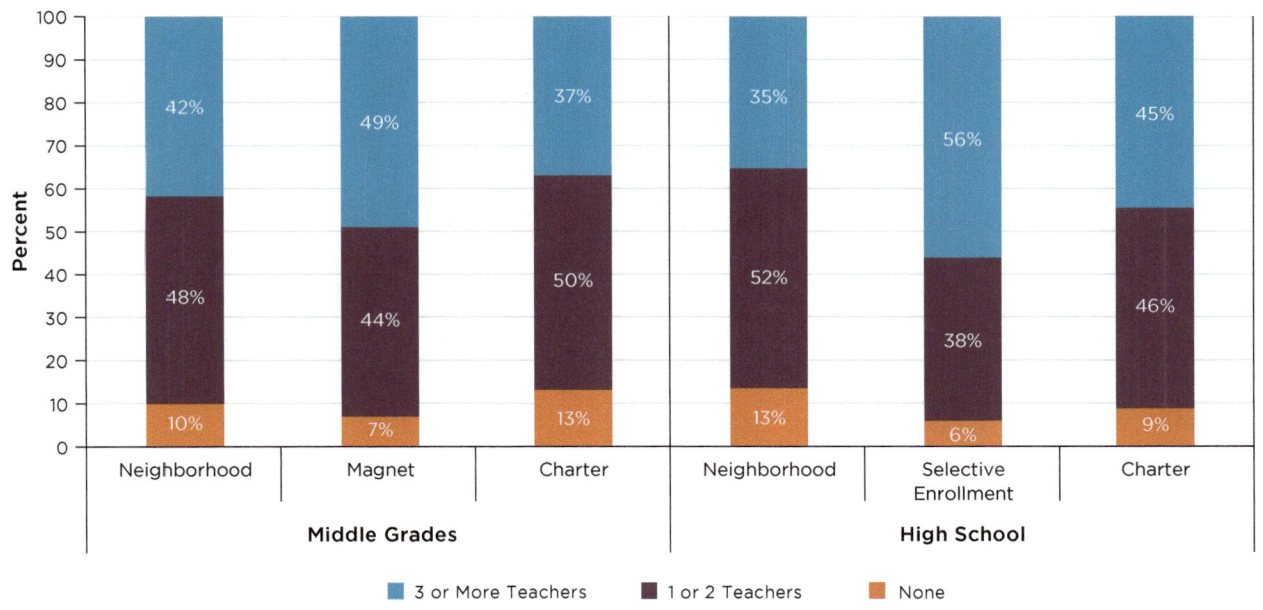

Note: Middle Grades (N = 57,728); High School (N = 63,257)

link exists because students who score higher on achievement tests facilitate more technology use by teachers and a more supportive school culture, or vice versa.

Teaching Digital Literacy

Not only do teachers' expectations and school-culture vary by school type, but so does the extent to which they are educating their students about digital literacy, a key component of effectively using the internet for academic purposes. Based on student responses in 2012 (**see Table A.1 in Appendix A** for complete survey items), those in magnet and selective enrollment schools are receiving more consistent messages about the importance of distinguishing between reliable and unreliable information on the internet (**Figure 11**). At the high school level, 56 percent of selective enrollment students say that at least three teachers talk to them about assessing the reliability of information they find online. This is in contrast to 35 percent of neighborhood high school students and 45 percent of charter high school students. Thus, students across the district are being exposed to teachers who provide differing amounts of instruction around the importance of critically analyzing information found online; students in magnet elementary and selective enrollment high schools have the dual benefit of teachers with higher expectations and teachers who provide more information supporting students' levels of digital literacy.

Links Between Teacher Use, School Culture, and Student Use of Technology

Our findings indicate similar trends across students and teachers. There is considerable variation in how frequently both students and teachers interact with technology, and the greater levels of use occur in magnet/selective enrollment schools and those with higher achievement. Given the similarities in these patterns, we analyzed whether greater technology use by teachers and a more supportive school culture for technology use occurred in the *same schools* where students reported higher use. We expected this to be the case, given prior CCSR research showing that technology use was higher in schools where there were more supports for that use.[22]

This relationship still holds 10 years later. Similar to our student findings, teachers use the internet to prepare their lessons, use technology for instructional delivery, and expect their students to use technology for their schoolwork more in schools with higher-achieving students and in selective enrollment high schools. Furthermore, teachers in these same types of schools feel more of a supportive culture for the use of technology and believe their school is doing a better job preparing students to be technologically literate. At both the elementary and high school level, our models **(see Model C in Tables C.1 and C.2 in Appendix C)** affirm that there is a significant relationship between the level of student use of technology and teacher technology use and expectation within the same schools.[23]

Although our models suggest that there are relationships between student and teacher use within a school, there may be other variables aside from school type that affect student use. For example, even within a single school type (e.g., charter schools), there can be a range of teacher use and expectations. The question is whether assessing these differences helps us better understand variations in student use of technology. Indeed, the differences in teacher use and school culture better explain how much students in those schools use technology—above and beyond school type, school-level achievement, and school-level social status.

Figure 12 shows that for high schools, individual student characteristics do not explain much of the school-by-school differences in use (the second bar). The third bar shows that when school characteristics are added into the model (school type, average school achievement, and average social status of the students in that school) they do explain some of the differences in how frequently students use technology across high schools, but also leave 52 percent of the variance unexplained. Finally, when we additionally take into account teacher use and school culture, another 18 percent of the original school-by-school differences

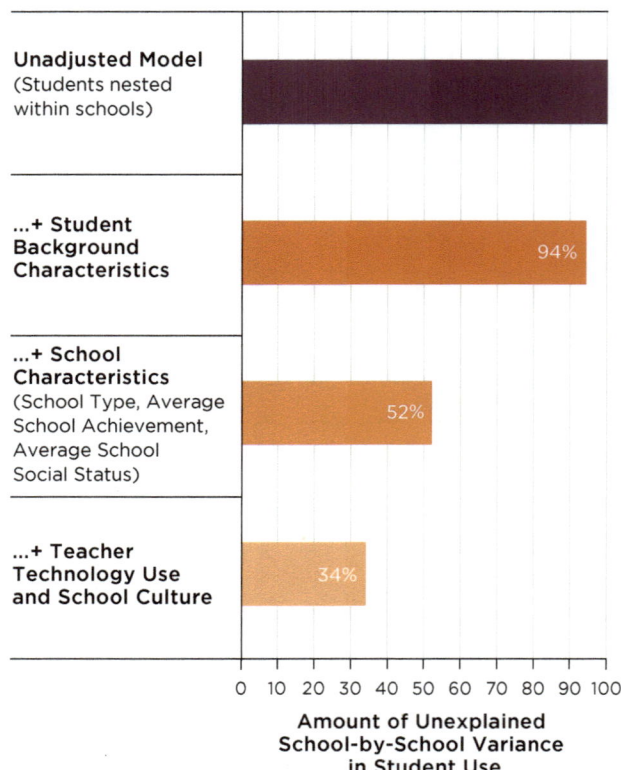

FIGURE 12

Teacher reports of technology use and school culture account for some of the unexplained school-by-school differences in student use (high school)

are explained, leaving only 34 percent unexplained. (**Table C.3** shows these relationships for both elementary and high schools.) Thus, knowing teacher practices and perceived level of school support helps us better understand some of the school-by-school differences in student use that remained at the end of Chapter 2.[24]

With the important role that school culture plays in students' technology use, we next turn to school leadership. We explore whether leadership affects technology use in schools by exhibiting high expectations, thereby reinforcing the importance of technology use and providing greater supports for teachers and students.

CHAPTER 3

Principals' Reports of Technology Use

Key Findings

- **More than 60 percent of principals** say they set high expectations for their teachers to integrate technology into their classrooms, but far fewer believe that their teachers are using technology to help students interact more with each other.
- **Roughly half of all principals** feel that their students are being prepared to be technologically literate; an additional 40 percent "somewhat" agree with this statement.
- **Teachers use technology more**, and feel more support for integrating technology into teaching and learning, in schools where principals say they have higher expectations for use.
- **Teachers also use technology more**, and feel more support for the use of technology, in schools where principals report fewer barriers to the use of computers and technology.

Previous studies have shown that technology leadership by the principal is a key component of whether computers and the internet are integrated into teaching and learning. The 2002 and 2007 CCSR reports on technology use in CPS showed that students and teachers used technology more in schools where leadership supported that use and in schools where principals themselves were more likely to use computers.[25] These findings are consistent with the research of Anderson and Dexter (2005), which found that in schools across the United States, technology leadership (including principals' use of email as a form of communication) was a key predictor of technology use and integration. Earlier CCSR findings also showed that barriers to technology use, as reported by principals, corresponded to overall use by students and teachers and teachers' expectations of student use for assignments.[26] Most of these findings were based on data collected nearly a decade ago. With the rapid changes in the growth of technology in schools, this chapter explores whether these same relationships exist in 2011. We first look at principals' expectations for technology use in their schools, and whether barriers to use have changed since 2005. Then, we ask whether these factors—principal expectations and technology barriers—are linked to student and teacher reports of technology use.[27]

What are Principals' Expectations for Use of Technology in Their Schools?

Most principals (60 percent) expect their teachers to integrate technology into their classrooms and teaching, and almost half strongly believe that their school is preparing their students to be technologically proficient. However, far fewer principals believe that their teachers are using technology to have students interact with one another – one important way that technology can be integrated into lessons, and one of the ways in which teachers at the postsecondary level utilize technology (**see Figure 13**, and **see Table A.5 in Appendix A** for exact wording of the survey items).

When we look more specifically at one of these items—whether their school is preparing their students to be technologically literate—the pattern is similar to student- and teacher-responses about technology: principals in selective enrollment or magnet schools are more likely to report that this is true, and charter school principals are least likely to report that their students are being prepared to be technologically literate (**see Figure 14**). More than 60 percent of principals in magnet/selective-enrollment schools agree with this statement "a great deal," while only 39 percent of charter school principals respond this way. On the positive side,

FIGURE 13

Though most principals expect integration of technology, far fewer believe teachers are using technology to have students interact

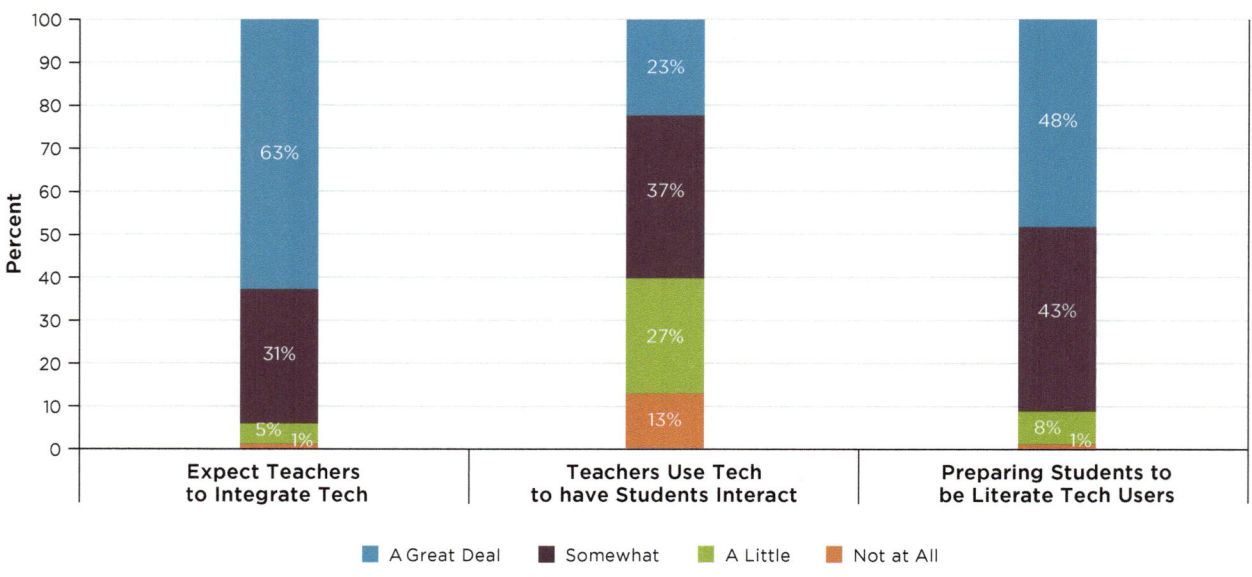

Note: N = 366

FIGURE 14

Principals in selective enrollment schools are most confident that their schools are preparing students to be technologically literate

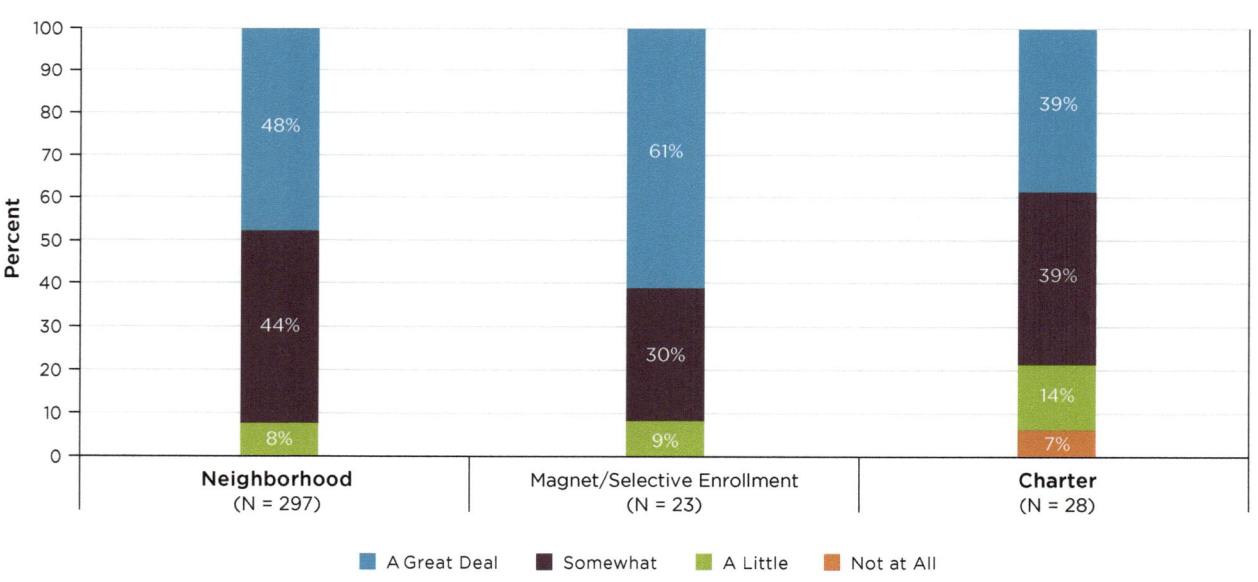

Note: N = 348

FIGURE 15

Most barriers to technology use declined slightly between 2005 and 2011

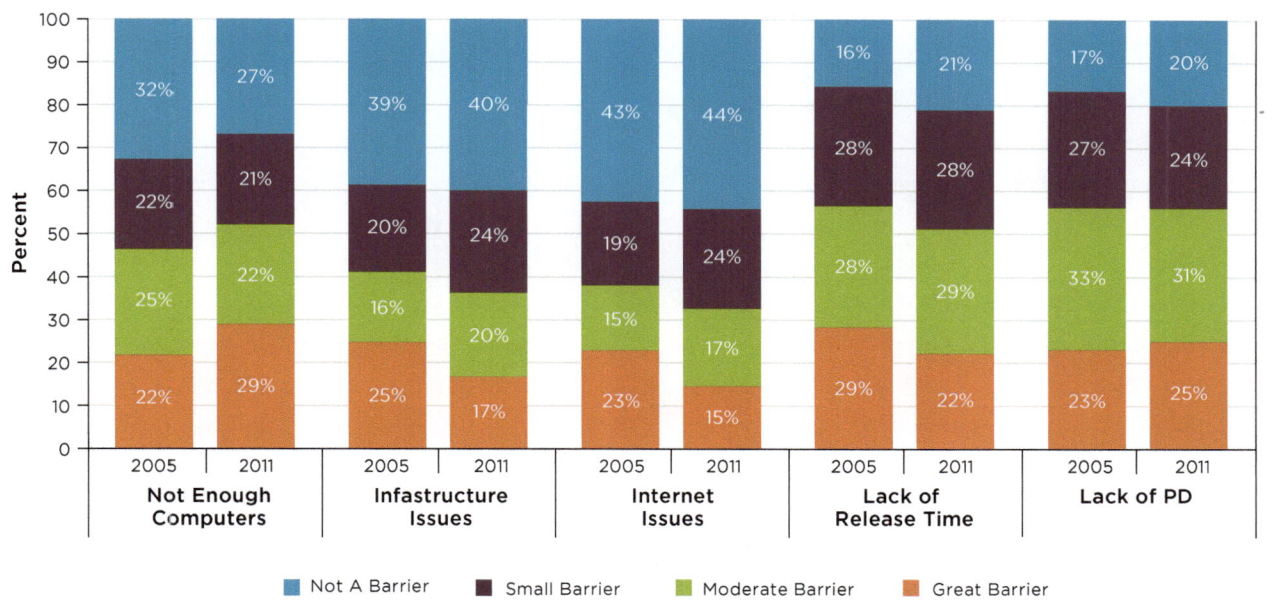

Note: These represent schools that responded to these items in both 2005 and 2011. Ns were between 200 and 205.

in all school types, over 80 percent of principals at least "somewhat" agreed that their schools are preparing their students to be technologically literate.

In earlier CCSR work, principals reported quite a few barriers to technology use that impacted how much technology was employed in their schools. The barriers did decrease from 2001 to 2005, partly due to a technology initiative that provided all high school teachers with laptops in their classrooms in 2001-02.[28] In our current survey, principals indicate barriers to technology use have continued to decline since 2005 (**Figure 15**), particularly with slight improvements in infrastructure issues, internet connection issues, and release time for teachers. However, barriers still exist. The lack of enough computers and lack of appropriate professional development (and release time for PD) appear to be the most common barriers to technology use in CPS schools. The fact that the availability of enough computers is a greater barrier now than in 2005 is likely a function of the increased one-to-one usage of computers in education.

Are Principals' Expectations of Technology Use Related to Student and Teacher Use?

In Chapter 3, we found that teacher use and the school culture around technology use were important indicators of student use within the school. Additionally, earlier research on technology use in Chicago showed that leadership was a crucial element of regular use of computers in schools; in schools where principals were more likely to use computers and report lower barriers, teachers were also integrating computer use into their work more.[29] Thus, we explore whether 10 years later, principals' expectations and their beliefs about barriers to technology use provide additional context around both teacher and student use. Our findings are similar to those of CCSR's earlier study.

For each outcome—teacher use and teacher-reported school culture—we ask whether principal reports of their own use and expectations, along with their reports of barriers to technology use in their school, explain some of the school-by-school differences.[30] In schools where teachers use and expect more technology use, principals also tend to have higher expectations for use and report fewer barriers to the use of technology (see **Appendix C, Table C.6; Table C.7** illustrates a similar finding for teacher-reported school culture).

In fact, understanding principals' levels of expectations and the barriers to technology use in their school helps explain additional differences in teacher use and school culture, above and beyond school type and composition. **Figure 16** shows that accounting for individual teacher characteristics (second bars) and school characteristics (e.g., school type, average achievement, and average social status of the students in the school [third bars]) leaves roughly 80 percent of the differences in teacher use and school culture unexplained. By capturing information about the level of expectations that principals hold for technology use and barriers to use in each school, we account for an *additional* 11 percent of the school-by-school differences in teacher use (**Figure 16; Table C.8 in Appendix C**). Similarly, principal reports also explain teachers' beliefs in whether there is a supportive school culture around the use of technology, by an *additional* 16 percent. Note, however, that almost 70 percent of the difference in teacher use and school culture across schools still remains unexplained. There are likely other variables we did not measure that would help us better understand what impacts teachers' technology use and expectations of use from their students.

Leadership Around Technology Use is Related to Student Technology Use

Recall that in Chapter 3 we found that teacher use and school culture explain some of the school-by-school differences in student use of technology. Here, we add to our understanding of which teachers are more or less likely to have higher expectations and use; we find that it is partially attributable to how school leadership approaches technology for learning. These findings, together with those presented in Chapter 3, indicate that we can better understand student technology use in a school by looking at a number of variables: (1) their school type and composition; (2) how much their teachers use and expect technology use in their school; and (3) how supportive their school culture is in supporting technology for instruction and learning. In an effort to better understand the difference in teachers' experiences, we add another variable and look at leadership.

In schools where principals do not have high expectations for the use of technology and report greater obstacles to integrating computers, teachers are less likely to feel the support for integration and to use computers themselves. By focusing on technology leadership, schools may see an improvement in the climate and may find that when structures are put into place, teachers and students are better supported in the use of technology.

FIGURE 16

Principal expectations and reports of school-level barriers to technology use account for some of the school-by-school differences in teacher use and school technology culture, above and beyond school type or student population

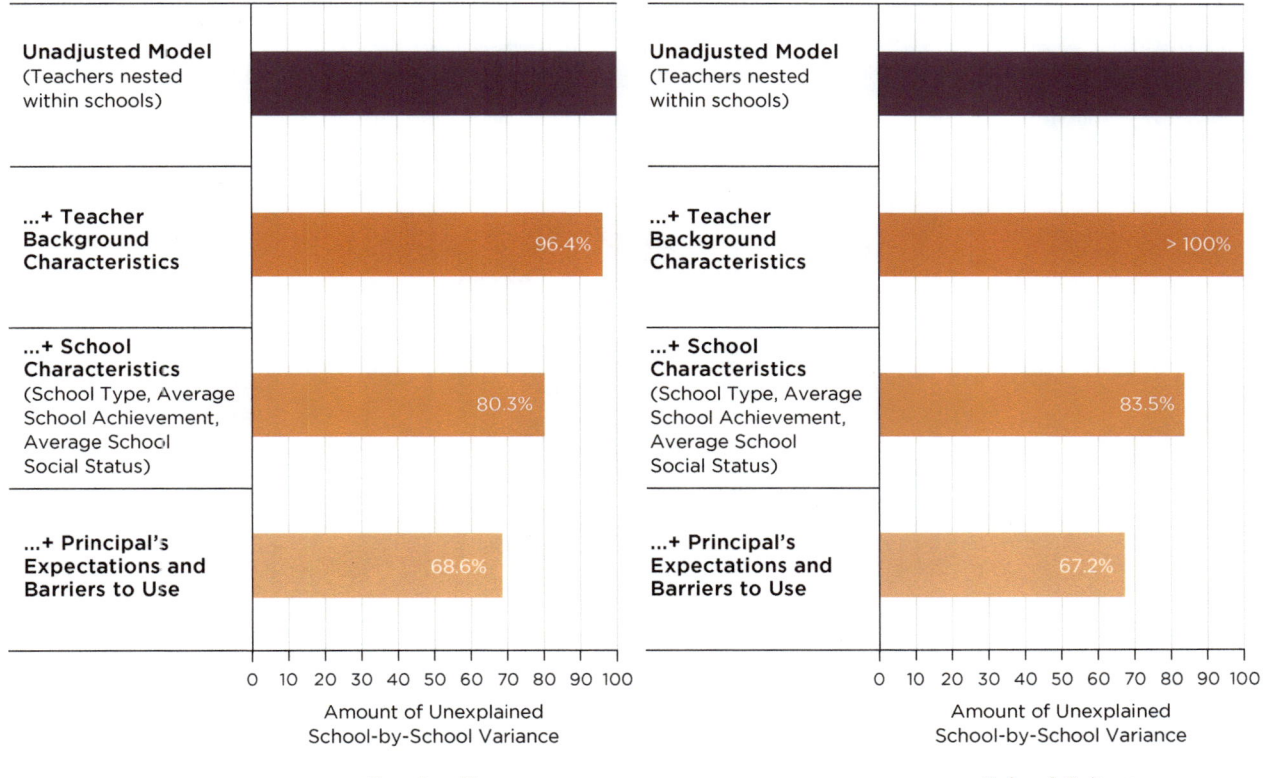

Chapter 3 | Principals' Reports about Technology Use

CHAPTER 4

Interpretive Summary

With more than 90 percent of teens using the internet[31], there is no doubt that technology use among youth continues to expand quickly. For students to be successful in college and the workplace, they need to develop technology skills that align with what they will experience after graduation.

These skills include being proficient enough not only to use technology to socialize with friends but also to use it in ways that enhance knowledge growth, promote exposure to new ideas, encourage problem solving, and support the development of technology skills expected for college and career success. Schools play a crucial role in supporting this development.

This report finds that most students in Chicago have access to computers and the internet outside of school, and report having people around them to turn to for help using these technologies. But what is lacking in students' experiences is the *expectation* that students regularly use technology for learning. To be sure, the frequency of use in and of itself does not ensure that the quality of use is high[32]; nevertheless, regular use is a prerequisite for higher-level interactions with technology. These expectations appear to be shaped by principals' and teachers' own use of, and perceived support for, the use of technology in their schools. We see variations in individual school culture of technology use across the district and across school types, which suggests students' opportunities to build technology skills may depend on which school they attend.

Levels of Technology Use Across the District Are Low

While there is currently no widespread consensus on how frequently students should engage with technology for school-related work, weekly use seems a minimum level of expectation in today's technological climate.[33] Since 2005, the use of computers for academic purposes in the Chicago Public Schools has grown more frequent, but it remains quite low even when we apply this minimal threshold of weekly use. Less than 60 percent of students use the internet regularly for school work, and even fewer students use computer programs to complete their assignments on a weekly basis—both of which are common uses of computers in today's colleges and working environments. Indeed, infrequent use of computers and the internet means that CPS students will have trouble meeting the emerging standards for technology literacy. The new Common Core State Standards, which are currently being applied across the country, call for technology use to be embedded in all aspects of students' learning.[34] In addition, the National Assessment of Educational Progress (NAEP) is now developing the first Technology and Engineering Literacy (TEL) Assessment, which will be administered in 2014. NAEP broadly defines technological and engineering literacy as the capacity to use, understand, and evaluate technology. The assessment will expect students to demonstrate skills in using technology to solve problems presented in realistic contexts and to communicate in a variety of ways, working both individually and in teams.[35]

When we consider a more engaged level of use, CPS

students appear even farther behind. Less than one-third of CPS students report regularly using technology to create original products for school, and another one-third never do. This is a missed opportunity for educators who could capitalize on students' interest in technology to facilitate active learning and encourage students to apply their knowledge to create something interesting and meaningful to them.[36]

Low levels of technology use in schools are not limited to students. While teachers report that they are quite comfortable with technology, and many report using the internet to prepare their lessons, far fewer regularly use computer programs to deliver instruction. Technology provides rich opportunities for conducting research, exploring ideas, and more deeply understanding the concepts being taught in class.[37] However, by limiting the use of computers and the internet to lesson preparation, teachers are not demonstrating to students the importance of learning how to use technologies or how to navigate the learning opportunities that technology affords. In addition, teachers are even less likely to expect that their students integrate the use of technology into their learning, and this was not because they believed their students lacked access. One potential way for teachers to encourage students to use technology for learning is to model this type of use. Teachers are more likely to get students to take advantage of these opportunities by setting an example and having clear expectations for their students' technology use; yet, both behaviors lag in CPS.

Technology Use Across Schools

The extent to which students use technology for learning is affected both by their individual characteristics and by the school they attend. While there are person-by-person differences in technology use, "typical" demographic characteristics (e.g., gender, social status, race/ethnicity, special education status, and retention) do not explain these well. Yet the amount of student technology use is related to the characteristics of the student's school.

We can find schools that exhibit higher levels of student and teacher use across all school types—neighborhood, magnet/selective enrollment, and charter schools. However, overall, technology use is higher in schools where there are higher-achieving students, and especially so in selective enrollment high schools. Over 45 percent of selective enrollment high schools (five of 11) are in the top quartile of both student use and teacher use, compared with just 6.3 percent (five of 79) of neighborhood high schools. And for most of our findings, charter schools look very similar to neighborhood schools, with teachers reporting lower expectations for use and principals reporting less confidence that they are preparing their students to be technologically literate compared to selective enrollment schools. This is an important finding given the prominence of charter schools in the current landscape of education policy and reform. It also may be a more difficult finding for districts to act on, given the autonomous role of charter schools.

The findings for both neighborhood and charter schools are disappointing. As a nation, we aspire for public schools to serve as an equalizer of opportunity; yet, these findings make clear that there are serious inequalities in the way that students use technologies across schools in the district. Indeed, when we consider that most students reported high rates of technology access at home, it appears as if schools might actually be intensifying, rather than eliminating, existing stratifications. However, schools can provide high-quality technology support, equalizing the experience of all students. The frequency of students', teachers', and principals' use of technologies is strongly linked to how much teachers and principals expect students to use technology, and how strong the school culture is around supporting the use of technology for teaching and learning. Thus, while students and teachers bring their own external experiences to the school, the support within the building can be quite powerful. Increasing teacher and principal use and expectations of technology show promise as viable methods to increasing student engagement with computers and the internet, particularly for the types of skills required under the Common Core State Standards and for students' future success.

It is encouraging that once we take into account the fact that students and teachers share the same school environment, neither being African American nor coming from a neighborhood with lower social status—

at both the individual level and when aggregated to the school level—is related to student use, teacher use or expectations, or the level of supportive culture for the use of technology in a school. In other words, the differences in technology use and expectations seem to be because of the differences in school experiences, *not* because of the level of poverty of the students attending that school. This suggests that students of all backgrounds are using software programs and the internet, so long as they are provided with the knowledge of how to use these tools and the opportunity to practice and work with them.

Further Research and Monitoring of Effective Technology Leadership in Schools

This research highlights the unequal use of technology across schools in Chicago. Some schools have students, teachers, and principals who use technology regularly as part of their communication, teaching, and learning, while others have students and staff who barely use computers at all. *This inequality deserves attention.* We know that technology use is higher in selective enrollment schools, but it also varies among neighborhood and charter schools. It is particularly critical to gain an understanding of how principals can best support the integration of technology into classrooms by teachers, and raise expectations so that students become regular users of computers and the internet.

Earlier work by CCSR outlined some of the particular steps principals took to support technology use in their school. These included applying for grants or finding ongoing funding, developing the capacity of their staff through professional development and professional learning communities, and setting the level of expectations of technology use (and exploration) within his/her school.[38] Work outside of Chicago has also suggested potential components of effective technology leadership.[39] These include, but are not limited to, establishing a technology committee; spending at least five days on technology planning; using email regularly for communication; creating a policy around staff development; maintaining discretionary authority over a school budget for technology; and receiving district support for technology expenses. Many of these components are highlighted in the International Society for Technology in Education's (ISTE) National Technology Standards for Administrators.[40]

While several studies have documented positive instances of technology leadership in schools[41], it is an area of focus that deserves more district attention. If CPS would like to eliminate the disparities across schools, it would be beneficial to further explore what effective technology leadership actually looks like inside CPS schools. To what extent are the ISTE standards for administrators being implemented? Beginning steps might include taking a closer look at STEM (Science, Technology, Engineering, and Mathematics) schools, or others that were designed to better support the use of technology. Are these schools succeeding in preparing their students to use technology to learn and, if so, what can we learn from them? In schools where standards are being implemented, how have principals and teachers successfully worked together to improve the integration of technology into their classrooms? How does a school with limited funding strategize to provide the professional development necessary to support principals' and teachers' use and integration of technology? Building the capacity to monitor changes over time, and sharing these findings with the district may support principals in becoming more effective technology leaders.

Technology Integration in the Future

Improving access to computers is not enough. Over the last decade, CPS and districts across the country have drastically increased their capabilities to provide students and teachers with laptops and internet access. However, our findings show that access alone does not necessarily lead to a large increase in use, consistent with earlier work emphasizing the importance of ongoing professional development and professional learning communities for teachers.[42] This notion will be important to remember as schools continue to stock their buildings with computers. Schools are under pressure to increase their technology supply, both for student use generally and for the administration of computer-based assessments. As the technology supply expands, it will be critical to measure how teachers are exploiting technology to build knowledge and skills and to offer more complex learning opportunities. In addition, as the Common Core State Standards are implemented across the country, expectations for student technology use will rise, placing an even greater burden on teachers and principals to find effective strategies for supporting technology use.

Our findings suggest that there are still significant challenges in preparing students to effectively use computers and other technologies. Especially in large urban districts such as Chicago, where there tends to be significant stratification in technology use from one school to another and across school types (e.g., selective enrollment, neighborhood), the call to action is no longer simply to provide students with computers and internet access. Rather, it is to raise the expectations for technology use in all schools, regardless of the academic skill-level of students within the school, so that all students have access to the experiences and knowledge required for post-school success. Given the increasing importance of technology literacy for functioning in most jobs, as well as for communicating, obtaining information and critiquing its veracity, and creating new products, there is a critical need to encourage technology integration into teaching and learning for all students.

References

ACT, Inc. (2011)
The EXPLORE Technical Manual. Iowa City, IA: Author. Retrieved from: http://www.act.org/explore/pdf/TechManual.pdf

Anderson, R.E., and Dexter, S. (2005)
School technology leadership: An empirical investigation of prevalence and effect. *Educational Administration Quarterly, 41*(1), 49-82.

Anthony, A.B. (2012)
Activity theory as a framework for investigating district-classroom system interactions and their influences on technology integration. *Journal of Research on Technology in Education, 44,* 335-356.

Bebell, D., O'Dwyer, L.M., Russell, M., and Hoffman, T. (2010)
Concerns, considerations, and new ideas for data collection and research in educational technology studies. *Journal of Research on Technology in Education, 43,* 29-52.

Coca, V. and Allensworth, E. (2007)
Trends in Access to Computing Technology and Its Use in Chicago Public Schools, 2001-2005. Chicago, IL: Consortium on Chicago School Research at the University of Chicago.

Dexter, S. (2011)
School technology leadership: Artifacts in systems of practice. *Journal of School Leadership, 21,* 166-189.

Goode, J. (2010)
Mind the gap: The digital dimension of college access. *The Journal of Higher Education, 81*(5), 583-618.

Hart, H., Allensworth, E., Lauen, D., and Gladden, R.M. (2002)
Educational Technology: Its Availability and Use in Chicago's Public Schools. Chicago, IL: Consortium on Chicago School Research at the University of Chicago.

Hillarious, M. and Milman, N. (April, 2012)
Learning in 1:1 laptop contexts: A review of the literature. Paper presented at the annual meeting of the American Education Research Association. Vancouver, BC, Canada.

International Society for Technology in Education (2009)
National Educational Technology Standards for Administrators (NETS-A). Retrieved on August 12, 2012, from http://www.iste.org/Libraries/PDFs/NETS-A_Standards.sflb.ashx

Lenhart, A., Purcell, K., Smith, A., and Zickuhr, K. (2010)
Social media & mobile internet use among teens and young adults. Pew Internet & American Life Project: Washington, DC. Retrieved from http://pewinternet.org/~/media//Files/Reports/2010/PIP_Social_Media_and_Young_Adults_Report_Final_with_toplines.pdf

Lie, J. (2010)
Quantity versus quality: A new approach to examine the relationship between technology use and student outcomes. *British Journal of Educational Technology, 41,* 433-472.

Moeller, B. and Reitzes, T. (2011)
Integrating technology with student centered learning. Quincy, MA: Nellie Mae Education Foundation. Retrieved from http://www.nmefdn.org/uploads/Integrating%20Tech%20with%20SCL.pdf

National Center for Education Statistics (2012)
National Assessment of Educational Progress: NAEP Technology and Engineering Literacy (TEL) Assessment. Retrieved on August 10, 2012, from http://nces.ed.gov/nationsreportcard/techliteracy/

National Governors Association Center for Best Practices, Council of Chief State School Officers (2010)
Common Core State Standards (English). Washington, DC: National Governors Association Center for Best Practices, Council of Chief State School Officers. Retrieved from http://www.corestandards.org/ELA-Literacy

Penuel, W.R., (2006)
Implementation and effects of one-to-one computer initiatives: A research synthesis. *Journal of Research on Technology in Education, 38,* 329-348.

Raudenbush, S.W. and Bryk, A.S. (2002)
Hierarchical linear models: Applications and data analysis methods (2nd ed.). Thousand Oaks, CA: Sage Publications.

Roschelle, J., Penuel, W. R., & Abrahamson, A. L. (2004).
The networked classroom. *Educational Leadership, 61,* 50-54.

Sax, L.J., Ceja, M., and Teranishi, R.T. (2001)
Technological preparedness among entering freshmen: The role of race, class, and gender. *Journal of Educational Computing Research, 24,* 363-383.

Warschauer, M. (2003).
Technology and social inclusion: Rethinking the digital divide. Cambridge, MA: The MIT Press.

Warschauer, M. and Matuchniak, T. (2010)
New technology and digital worlds: Analyzing evidence of equity in access, use, and outcomes. *Review of Research in Education, 34,* 179-225.

Appendix A
Survey Items

TABLE A.1

2012 Student Survey Items

Q1. How do you connect to the internet at home?

RESPONSE CATEGORIES:
Yes, No

A. Through a dial-up telephone line.

B. Through a high-speed connection such as cable or DSL (includes cable, DSL, satellite, fiber optic, T-1).

C. Only through a cell-phone plan (includes 3G and 4G).

D. I do not connect to the internet at home.

E. Not sure.

Q2. Consider this situation: Suppose you had a school project and you needed help using the computer to finish the project.

RESPONSE CATEGORIES:
None, 1 or 2 People, More Than 3 People

A. How many people do you have IN SCHOOL who can help you?

B. How many people do you have OUTSIDE OF SCHOOL who can help you?

Q3. How much do you agree with the following statements?

RESPONSE CATEGORIES:
Strongly Disagree, Disagree, Neutral, Agree, Strongly Agree

A. I prefer finding information online rather than offline.

B. I remember more information when I read things on screen than when I read things in print.

Q4. How many of your teachers have explained how to tell whether or not information on the internet is reliable (meaning you can trust the information)?

RESPONSE CATEGORIES:
None, 1 or 2, 3 or More

TABLE A.2

2011 Student Measure: Student Technology Use

The following questions ask about your use of technology FOR SCHOOL, including classes and after-school programs:

RESPONSE CATEGORIES:
Never, Once or Twice a Semester, Once or Twice a Month, Once or Twice a Week, Almost Every or Every Day

Q1. I use technology to make something new and creative (like a movie, website, podcast, blog, graphic design, game design) for either a class or another school-based program.

Q2. I use the internet to find information for school assignments.

Q3. I use computer programs, such as Excel, PowerPoint, or Publisher, to complete school assignments or projects.

The following questions ask about your use of technology OUTSIDE OF SCHOOL:

RESPONSE CATEGORIES:
Never, Once or Twice a Semester, Once or Twice a Month, Once or Twice a Week, Almost Every or Every Day

Q4. I use technology to make something new and creative (like a movie, website, podcast, blog, graphic design, game design) outside of school.

Q5. I use technology to connect with others about social or community issues when I am outside of school.

Q6. I use the internet to look up information I need outside of school (not including the use of social networking sites like Facebook or Twitter).

Q7. I use computer programs, such as Excel, PowerPoint, or Publisher, outside of school.

TABLE A.3

2005 Student Survey Items

Q1. This year, how often do you use a computer AT SCHOOL for the following things:

RESPONSE CATEGORIES:
Never, Once or Twice a Semester, Once or Twice a Month, Once or Twice a Week, Almost Every or Every Day

A. Analyse or graph data (in Excel, for example)?

B. Create presentations (in PowerPoint, for example)?

C. Do research using the internet?

TABLE A.4

2011 Teacher Survey Measures

Measure 1: Teacher Use

How often do you:

RESPONSE CATEGORIES:
Never/No Access, Once or Twice a Semester, Once or Twice a Month, Weekly, Almost Daily or More

Q1. Expect students to use computers or other technologies in completing their class work or assignments?

Q2. Use a computer and/or the internet outside of class for such activities as lesson preparation, getting ideas, or examples of best practice?

Q3. Incorporate software beyond word processors (such as PowerPoint, video clips, live internet searches, music or audio clips, or similar media) when you deliver lessons?

Measure 2: Teacher-Reported Culture

Please indicate the degree to which:

RESPONSE CATEGORIES:
Not at All/No Access, A Little, Somewhat, Very Much

Q1. Your school is preparing its students to be proficient in the use of technology.

Q2. Your school's culture encourages technology usage for instruction.

Q3. Your school's culture encourages technology usage for communication with students.

Q4. Your school's culture encourages technology usage for communication with students' families.

TABLE A.5

2011 Principal Survey Items and Measures

Measure 1: Principal Expectations

To what extent:

RESPONSE CATEGORIES:
Not at All, A Little, Somewhat, A Great Deal

Q1. Do you expect teachers at your school to integrate technology into their classroom?

Q2. Is your school preparing students to be literate technology users?

Q3. Do your teachers use technology (e.g., creating classroom listservs) to have students interact with each other.

Measure 2: Barriers to Technology Use

Please indicate to what extent, if any, each of the following is a barrier to teachers' use of school computers or the internet for instruction:

RESPONSE CATEGORIES:
Not a Barrier, Small Barrier, Moderate Barrier, Great Barrier

Q1. Not enough computers.

Q2. Infrastructure issues (e.g., wiring, asbestos, unreliable wireless).

Q3. Internet or networking issues (not enough internet connections, incompatible networks, etc.).

Q4. Lack of release time for teachers to learn/practice/plan ways to use computers or the Internet.

Q5. Lack of appropriate professional development on how to integrate computing technology into curriculum.

Appendix B
Methods

Survey Data Collection

CCSR has been administering biennial surveys to students in the sixth through twelfth grades, teachers, and principals in the Chicago Public Schools since 1992. Beginning in 2011, student and teacher surveys began to be administered annually. The surveys used for this report were administered online between March and April of 2011 and 2012. The responses give CCSR data on school climate, school organizational structure, parental support, perceptions of school, and teacher-student relationships.

Creation of Survey Measures Using Rasch Analyses

We used Rasch Analysis to produce measures from multiple items on the 2011 survey that are more comprehensive and reliable than individual items. The Rasch approach permits the creation of latent variables (e.g., Students' Technology Use, Principal Expectations) that are conceptually and empirically cohesive. Using items that relate to the same characteristic, a scale was constructed reflecting the relative "difficulty" (the likelihood that respondents will agree with a given item) of each item.

The decision to omit or to include an item in a measure was based on the fit statistic, which has an expected value of 1 and is calculated by taking the mean squared deviations between the expected and observed values for that item. Items for which the fit statistic was greater than 1.3 were excluded. The scales were also evaluated using the person reliability statistic (the ratio of adjusted standard deviation to the root mean square error computed over the persons) which is approximately equivalent to Cronbach's alpha.

The Rasch measures are created on a logit scale. Since each measure represents a different latent characteristic, it is inappropriate to compare scores across measures—if a school has a mean score of 0.50 on Teacher-reported Culture and a mean score of 1.0 on Teacher Use, it does not necessarily mean that the school is "better" on Teacher Use than it is on Teacher-reported Culture.

All measures in this report were created using Rasch analyses on responses to the 2011 survey. Reliabilities for each of our measures are provided in **Table B.1** below.

TABLE B.1

Survey Measure Reliabilities	
Student Technology Use	0.77
Teacher Use	0.60
Teacher-Reported Culture	0.85
Principal Expectations	0.64

Analyses Using Hierarchical Linear Models

Characteristics Included in Models

Student characteristics included in the models are those shown below, under the basic model structure section. This included gender, race/ethnicity, special education status, being old for grade, and grade level, their achievement scores, and an indicator of students' social status based on the occupations and education levels of residents in their neighborhood. Social status is calculated based on the census block group in which each student lives, and includes mean level of education of adults and the percentage of employed persons who work as managers or professionals based on 2010 census data. These are then standardized across all students in the district. Thus, a higher value corresponds to a higher block-level social status. School-level characteristics included were school-level means of social status and student achievement, and the type of school (neighborhood, magnet/selective enrollment, or charter).

Achievement was defined differently for elementary and high school models. For elementary models, achievement is the Illinois Standard Achievement Test (ISAT) reading score of all students from the prior year, standardized within year and grade. For high school models, achievement is each student's ninth-grade EXPLORE score,[43] standardized across the high school population, and centered around the mean for selective enrollment students or non-selective enrollment students. This allowed us to measure the impact of being in a selective enrollment high school, even though by fact they admit the highest-scoring students across CPS. Measures of social status were also standardized. All variables were entered into the model grand-mean-centered.

Basic Model Structure

We employed a multi-level (HLM) measurement model where students or teachers were nested within schools. Our student and teacher models also adjusted for measurement error at level 1. Each student or teacher measure was divided by the person specific standard error for that measure in order to account for the number and consistency of the responses. Levels 2 and 3 represent traditional levels 1 and 2—students/teachers nested within schools. The final models used to predict student use of technology in elementary schools are shown below. At the high school level, there were two differences: (1) there were dummies for grades 10, 11, and 12 instead of for grades seven and eight; and (2) standardized scores were included for the ninth-grade EXPLORE test instead of the ISAT Reading test.

LEVEL-1 MODEL

$(\text{Tech\_Measure\_Score}_{ijk} = \pi_{1jk} * (\text{Standard Error}_{ijk}) + e_{ijk}$

LEVEL-2 MODEL

$\pi_{1jk} = \beta_{10k} + \beta_{11k} * (\text{SPECIAL\_ED}_{jk}) + \beta_{12k} * (\text{BLACK}_{jk}) + \beta_{13k} * (\text{NATIVE\_AM}_{jk}) + \beta_{14k} * (\text{ASIAN}_{jk}) + \beta_{15k} * (\text{LATINO}_{jk}) + \beta_{16k} * (\text{MULTI}_{jk}) + \beta_{17k} * (\text{MALE}_{jk}) + \beta_{18k} * (\text{OLD\_FOR\_GRADE}_{jk}) + \beta_{19k} * (\text{GRADE7}_{jk}) + \beta_{110k} * (\text{GRADE8}_{jk}) + \beta_{111k} * (\text{Z\_SOCIAL\_STATUS}_{jk}) + \beta_{112k} * (\text{Z\_READING}_{jk}) + r_{1jk}$

LEVEL-3 MODEL

$\beta_{10k} = \gamma_{100} + \gamma_{101}(\text{AV\_Z\_SOCIAL\_STATUS}_{k}) + \gamma_{102}(\text{AV\_Z\_READING}_{k}) + \gamma_{103}(\text{SELECTIVE\_ENROLLMENT}_{k}) + \gamma_{104}(\text{CHARTER}_{k}) + u_{10k}$

$\beta_{11k} = \gamma_{110}$
$\beta_{12k} = \gamma_{120}$
$\beta_{13k} = \gamma_{130}$
$\beta_{14k} = \gamma_{140}$
$\beta_{15k} = \gamma_{150}$
$\beta_{16k} = \gamma_{160}$
$\beta_{17k} = \gamma_{170}$
$\beta_{18k} = \gamma_{180}$
$\beta_{19k} = \gamma_{190}$
$\beta_{110k} = \gamma_{1100}$
$\beta_{111k} = \gamma_{1110}$
$\beta_{112k} = \gamma_{1120}$

In all models, all predictors were centered on the grand mean. Therefore the interpretation of the intercept is for the average student attending the average school in CPS, individually calculated for elementary and high school models.

Variations to Basic Models

For models that include principal measures as predictors, the elementary and high schools are combined in the same model (due to small numbers). in these models, achievement was calculated and standardized within elementary and high schools and then combined into one model. A separate predictor for level (elementary vs. high school) captures the overall difference between elementary and high schools.

When using other measures as predictors rather than outcomes (e.g., teacher measure to predict student measure), the measures were first standardized.

Appendix C
Tables from HLM and Regression Analyses

TABLE C.1

Student Technology Use, Elementary Schools (Hierarchical Linear Models)

	Model A (Level 1 Predictors Only)		Model B (Level 1 and Level 2 Predictors)		Model C (Level 1 and Level 2 Predictors with Teacher Measures)	
	β	SE	β	SE	β	SE
INTERCEPT	-0.003	0.009	-0.006	0.008	-0.006	0.008
School Characteristics						
Teacher Use of Technology					0.079***	0.020
Teacher Reported School Culture					0.071***	0.017
Mean Social Status			0.008	0.014	0.019	0.013
Mean ISAT Reading			0.131***	0.026	0.067**	0.026
Selective Enrollment			0.037	0.035	0.061	0.034
Charter			-0.009	0.059	-0.006	0.051
Student Characteristics						
Social Status	-0.001	0.004	-0.007	0.004	-0.007	0.004
Male	-0.034***	0.006	-0.034***	0.006	-0.034***	0.006
Special Ed Status	-0.072***	0.012	-0.077***	0.012	-0.077***	0.012
African American	0.007	0.015	0.028	0.015	0.024	0.015
Native American	-0.079	0.041	-0.070	0.041	-0.074	0.041
Asian	0.054**	0.018	0.055**	0.019	0.052**	0.019
Latino	-0.065***	0.012	-0.056***	0.012	-0.057***	0.012
Multi-Racial	-0.014	0.026	-0.011	0.026	-0.015	0.026
Old for Grade	0.011	0.009	0.012	0.009	0.012	0.009
Grade 7	0.044***	0.011	0.044***	0.011	0.045***	0.011
Grade 8	0.073***	0.012	0.073***	0.012	0.075***	0.012
ISAT Reading	0.001	0.005	-0.002	0.005	-0.003	0.005

* <= .05; ** <= .01; *** <= .001

Notes:
1. Social status was standardized around a mean of 0 and standard deviation of 1 within the elementary (middle-grade) students enrolled in CPS for 2010-2011.
2. The reference category for race is White and the reference categories for middle and high school grades are sixth and ninth grade, respectively.
3. Teacher measures were standardized around a mean of 0 and a standard deviation of 1, within elementary and high school teachers who had scores for this measure.

Ns: Model A = 57,178 students, 464 schools; **Model B** = 57,151 students, 452 schools; **Model C** = 56,372 students, 446 schools

TABLE C.2

Student Technology Use, High Schools (Hierarchical Linear Models)

	Model A (Level 1 Predictors Only)		Model B (Level 1 and Level 2 Predictors)		Model C (Level 1 and Level 2 Predictors with Teacher Measures)	
	β	SE	β	SE	β	SE
INTERCEPT	0.114***	0.016	0.107***	0.012	0.106***	0.010
School Characteristics						
Teacher Use of Technology					0.093*	0.036
Teacher Reported School Culture					0.107***	0.029
Mean Social Status			0.000	0.026	-0.002	0.023
Mean Entering EXPLORE			0.150***	0.031	0.111***	0.028
Selective Enrollment			0.308***	0.043	0.235***	0.041
Charter			0.094**	0.035	0.112***	0.030
Student Characteristics						
Social Status	0.006	0.004	0.005	0.004	0.005	0.004
Male	-0.043***	0.007	-0.044***	0.007	-0.044***	0.007
Special Ed Status	-0.058***	0.013	-0.057***	0.013	-0.059***	0.013
African American	0.024	0.018	0.034	0.019	0.037*	0.018
Native American	-0.129**	0.049	-0.127**	0.049	-0.128**	0.049
Asian	0.109***	0.022	0.107***	0.022	0.106***	0.022
Latino	-0.043*	0.018	-0.040*	0.018	-0.040*	0.018
Multi-Racial	0.044	0.037	0.045	0.037	0.041	0.037
Old for Grade	-0.027**	0.010	-0.024*	0.010	-0.025*	0.010
Grade 10	-0.020	0.015	-0.020	0.015	-0.021	0.015
Grade 11	0.066***	0.015	0.066***	0.015	0.065***	0.015
Grade 12	0.159***	0.019	0.160***	0.019	0.158***	0.019
9th grade EXPLORE	0.035***	0.007	0.034***	0.007	0.034***	0.007

* <= .05; ** <= .01; *** <= .001

Notes:
1. Social status was standardized around a mean of 0 and standard deviation of 1 within the high school students enrolled in CPS for 2010-2011.
2. The reference category for race is White and the reference categories for middle and high school grades are sixth and ninth grade, respectively.
3. Teacher measures were standardized around a mean of 0 and a standard deviation of 1, within elementary and high school teachers who had scores for this measure."

Ns: Model A = 49,527 students, 130 schools; **Model B** = 49,356 students, 123 schools; **Model C** = 48,942 students, 120 schools

TABLE C.3

Teacher Technology Use (Hierarchical Linear Models)

Elementary School	β	SE	High School	β	SE
INTERCEPT	0.939***	0.023	**INTERCEPT**	1.078***	0.031
School Characteristics			**School Characteristics**		
Mean Social Status	-0.047	0.037	Mean Social Status	-0.023	0.055
Mean ISAT Reading	0.316***	0.074	Mean Entering EXPLORE	0.157*	0.077
Magnet	-0.004	0.106	Selective Enrollment	0.485***	0.094
Charter	-0.140	0.146	Charter	0.037	0.105
Teacher Characteristics			**Teacher Characteristics**		
Male	0.234***	0.045	Male	0.023	0.046
Latino	0.037	0.046	Latino	0.134	0.085
African American	0.140***	0.043	African American	0.048	0.063
Native American	0.111	0.080	Native American	0.010	0.139
Asian	0.109	0.080	Asian	-0.023	0.101
Master's Degree	0.060	0.039	Master's Degree	0.052	0.058
Advanced Degree	0.163***	0.041	Advanced Degree	0.058	0.062
Computer	Not included		Computer	1.351***	0.271
English	Not included		English	-0.031	0.110
Math	Not included		Math	-0.280**	0.108
Science	Not included		Science	0.131	0.099
Social Studies	Not included		Social Studies	0.086	0.107
Language	Not included		Language	-0.314*	0.134
1-3 Years	0.016	0.100	1-3 Years	0.235	0.144
4-5 Years	-0.025	0.098	4-5 Years	0.208	0.129
6-10 Years	-0.078	0.094	6-10 Years	0.139	0.132
11-15 Years	-0.130	0.097	11-15 Years	0.120	0.145
More than 15 Years	-0.192*	0.097	More than 15 Years	0.089	0.146

* <= .05; ** <= .01; *** <= .001

Notes:
1. Social status was standardized around a mean of 0 and standard deviation of 1 within the elementary and high school sample, then averaged up to the school level.
2. Our reference category for teacher experience is less than one year experience. For subject taught, the comparisons are between the subject entered and all omitted subjects (including art, music, drama; physical education; special education; and vocational, business). We look at whether teachers at the high school level taught one of the core course subjects or taught computer classes.

Ns Elementary = 5,467 teachers, 436 schools; **Ns High School** = 1,736 teachers, 115 schools

TABLE C.4

Teacher Reported School Culture (Hierarchical Linear Models)

Elementary School	β	SE	High School	β	SE
INTERCEPT	3.105***	0.079	**INTERCEPT**	2.694***	0.136
School Characteristics			**School Characteristics**		
Mean Social Status	-0.092	0.126	Mean Social Status	-0.242	0.240
Mean ISAT Reading	1.674***	0.259	Mean Entering EXPLORE	1.238***	0.325
Magnet	-0.269	0.438	Selective Enrollment	1.992***	0.360
Charter	-0.579	0.401	Charter	0.285	0.404
Teacher Characteristics			**Teacher Characteristics**		
Computer	Not included		Computer	0.262	0.862
English	Not included		English	-0.633*	0.286
Math	Not included		Math	0.075	0.317
Science	Not included		Science	-0.168	0.320
Social Studies	Not included		Social Studies	-0.162	0.325
Language	Not included		Language	0.193	0.378
1-3 Years	0.099	0.244	1-3 Years	0.392	0.346
4-5 Years	0.205	0.249	4-5 Years	0.713*	0.359
6-10 Years	0.175	0.024	6-10 Years	0.665	0.342
11-15 Years	0.417	0.248	11-15 Years	1.425***	0.340
More than 15 Years	0.997***	0.238	More than 15 Years	1.581***	0.372

* <= .05; ** <= .01; *** <= .001

Notes:
1. Social status was standardized around a mean of 0 and standard deviation of 1 within the elementary and high school sample, then averaged up to the school level.
2. Our reference category for teacher experience is less than one year experience. For subject taught, the comparisons are between the subject entered and all omitted subjects (including art, music, drama; physical education; special education; and vocational, business) . We look at whether teachers at the high school level taught one of the core course subjects or taught computer classes.

Ns Elementary = 6,016 teachers, 436 schools; **Ns High School** = 1,854 teachers, 115 schools

TABLE C.5

Variance Explained by the Addition of Variables to Student Models

Model		Student-Level Variance	School-Level Variance	Total Variance	Percent Variance at the School Level	Remaining Student-Level Variance	Remaining School-Level Variance
Elementary School							
A	Unadjusted Student Model	0.275	0.027	0.302	8.9%	**100%**	**100%**
B	...+ Student Characteristics (gender, race, grade, achievement, SES, retainment, special education status)	0.272	0.026	0.297	8.7%	**98.9%**	**98.6%**
C	...+ School Characteristics (school type, average achievement, average social status)	0.272	0.022	0.294	7.6%	**98.9%**	**82.9%**
With Teacher Predictors							
D	Model C + Teacher Use Only	0.271	0.019	0.290	6.5%	**98.7%**	**69.6%**
E	Model C + Technology Culture Only	0.271	0.019	0.290	6.5%	**98.7%**	**70.4%**
F	Model C + Technology Culture and Teacher Use	0.271	0.018	0.289	6.2%	**98.7%**	**66.3%**
Model		Student-Level Variance	School-Level Variance	Total Variance	Percent Variance at the School Level	Remaining Student-Level Variance	Remaining School-Level Variance
High School							
G	Unadjusted student model	0.319	0.030	0.349	8.6%	**100%**	**100%**
H	...+ Student Characteristics (gender, race, grade, achievement, SES, retainment, special education status)	0.310	0.029	0.339	8.4%	**97.3%**	**94.4%**
I	...+ School Characteristics (school type, average achievement, average social status)	0.310	0.016	0.326	4.8%	**97.3%**	**52.3%**
With Teacher Predictors							
J	Model C + Teacher Use Only	0.311	0.012	0.323	3.7%	**97.4%**	**39.2%**
K	Model C + Technology Culture Only	0.311	0.011	0.322	3.5%	**97.4%**	**37.3%**
L	Model C + Technology Culture and Teacher Use	0.311	0.010	0.321	3.2%	**97.4%**	**34.4%**

N's: Model A (59,517 students, 464 schools); **Model B** (57,178 students, 464 schools); **Model C** (57,151 students, 452 schools); **Models D - F** (56,372 students, 446 schools); **Model G** (54,341 students, 140 schools); **Model H** (49,527 students, 130 schools); **Model I** (49,407 students, 123 schools); **Models J-L** (48,961 students, 120 schools)

TABLE C.6
Relationship between Principal Measures and Teacher Use of Technology

	β	SE
INTERCEPT	0.953***	0.024
Level 2 (School)		
Principals' Expectations	0.133***	0.024
Barriers to Technology Use	-0.061**	0.022
High School	0.426**	0.183
Mean Social Status	-0.010	0.026
Mean Prior Ability	0.110***	0.032
Magnet/Selective Enrollment	0.212*	0.105
Charter	-0.089	0.122
Level 1 (Teacher)		
Male	0.159***	0.045
Latino	0.015	0.048
African American	0.138**	0.046
Native American	0.083	0.085
Asian	0.002	0.080
Master's Degree	0.018	0.040
Advanced Degree	0.129**	0.043
Computer	1.507***	0.443
English	-0.131	0.195
Math	-0.499**	0.177
Science	0.029	0.150
Social Studies	0.073	0.173
Language	-0.482*	0.193
1-3 Years	0.077	0.109
4-5 Years	0.130	0.104
6-10 Years	0.019	0.102
11-15 Years	-0.042	0.103
More than 15 Years	-0.082	0.105

* <= .05; ** <= .01; *** <= .001

Ns = 4,147 teachers, 334 schools

TABLE C.7
Relationship between Principal Measures and Teacher Reported School Culture

	β	SE
INTERCEPT	3.092***	0.083
Level 2 (School)		
Principals' Expectations	0.480***	0.088
Barriers to Technology Use	-0.192*	0.091
High School	0.406	0.322
Mean Social Status	0.061	0.086
Mean Prior Ability	0.646***	0.112
Magnet/Selective Enrollment	0.428	0.424
Charter	-0.660	0.342
Level 1 (Teacher)		
Computer	0.656	1.250
English	-0.537	0.396
Math	0.018	0.351
Science	-0.009	0.414
Social Studies	-0.069	0.376
Language	-0.027	0.421
1-3 Years	0.184	0.260
4-5 Years	0.398	0.278
6-10 Years	0.440	0.262
11-15 Years	0.636*	0.270
More than 15 Years	1.206***	0.266

* <= .05; ** <= .01; *** <= .001

Ns = 4,575 teachers, 334 schools

TABLE C.8

Teacher Variance Accounted for by Principal Expectations and Technology Barriers

Model		Teacher-Level Variance	School-Level Variance	Total Variance	Percent Variance at the School Level	Remaining Teacher-Level Variance	Remaining School-Level Variance
Outcome: Teacher Use							
A	Unadjusted teacher model	0.600	0.109	0.709	15.4%	**100%**	**100%**
B	...+ Teacher characteristics (gender, race, educational attainment, experience, and subject taught)	0.565	0.105	0.670	15.7%	**94.1%**	**96.4%**
C	...+ School characteristics (school type, average achievement, average social status)	0.563	0.088	0.650	13.5%	**93.8%**	**80.3%**
D	...+ Principal's Expectations and Barriers to Technology Use	0.595	0.075	0.670	11.2%	**99.2%**	**68.6%**
Outcome: Teacher-Reported School Culture							
E	Unadjusted teacher model	7.613	2.217	9.831	22.6%	**100%**	**100%**
F	...+ Teacher characteristics (experience and subject taught)	7.286	2.287	9.573	23.9%	**95.7%**	**103.2%**
G	...+ School characteristics (school type, average achievement, average social status)	7.283	1.851	4.138	44.7%	**95.7%**	**83.5%**
H	...+ Principal's Expectations and Barriers to Technology Use	7.284	1.491	8.775	17.0%	**95.7%**	**67.2%**

Ns: Model A (9,343 teachers; 649 schools); **Model B** (7,615 teachers; 645 schools); **Model C** (7,349 teachers; 608 schools); **Model D** (4,507 teachers; 342 schools); **Model E** (9,422 teachers; 649 schools); **Model F** (8,317 teachers; 646 schools); **Model G** (8,029 teachers; 609 schools); **Model H** (4,928 teachers; 342 schools)

Endnotes

Introduction

1. NGA and CCSSO (2010).
2. Moeller and Reitzes (2011).
3. Sax, Ceja, and Teranishi (2001).
4. Goode (2010).
5. Hart, Allensworth, Lauen, and Gladden (2002).
6. Coca and Allensworth (2007).
7. Raudenbush and Bryk (2002).

Chapter 1

8. Warschauer (2003); Warschauer and Matuchniak (2010).
9. Lenart, Purcell, Smith, and Zickhur (2010).
10. There are some differences in access to high-speed internet across groups of students. In particular, a higher proportion, or about 85 percent, of white and Asian students (who are also the students least likely to be eligible for free or reduced-price lunch) have access to high-speed internet compared with about 72 to 75 percent of other students.
11. Hillarious and Millman (2012).
12. We did not include Microsoft Word because we believed that most students were likely to be using word processing software on a regular basis, but less likely to use other software that would be expected for use in college and the workforce. Therefore, we asked about programs that were slightly higher-level than Word.
13. Penuel (2006).
14. Descriptive analyses conducted by the authors on 2005 CCSR survey data.
15. Figures 4 and 5 display the responses of high school students to the item that asked how frequently they use the internet to find information for school assignments. We chose this item because it fell in the middle of the difficulty range in our Rasch analyses when creating our overall measure of student technology use (see Appendix B for further details on methods). These results were similar to the item that asked about using computer programs, but patterns were muted or disappeared for the item asking about making something new and creative for school, where overall responses indicated lower frequency of use. The results for internet use and making something new and creative were similar for middle-grade and high school students; the differences in student use of computer programs by student background characteristics were in the same direction but muted for middle-grade students.
16. For high school students, achievement is measured using ninth-grade EXPLORE scores. EXPLORE is taken by all ninth-graders in CPS and is the point of entry into the secondary school level of ACT's College and Career Readiness System, a series of assessments that includes EXPLORE, PLAN, and ACT (ACT, 2011). In the models presented in Appendix C, achievement for elementary students is their prior year's Illinois Standard Achievement Test (ISAT) score.
17. The outcome in our HLM model is the measure of overall technology use. See Table A.1 for all the items included in this measure. In addition, our HLM models use a measure of social status instead of free or reduced-price lunch status; this is a more sensitive measure of socio-economic status because 85 percent of all CPS students receive free or reduced-price lunch.
18. Model A in tables C.1 and C.2 displays findings from HLM models that only include student characteristics. We also ran those same models excluding achievement (ISAT Reading for elementary students and ninth-grade EXPLORE for high school students). Being African American and having lower social status continued to be insignificant predictors of student technology use even when we excluded student achievement at level 1. Thus, achievement is not what explains the differences by race seen in Figure 4.

Chapter 2

19. While we see that at the school level, student use and teacher use are significantly related, we cannot link students directly to their teachers, so we cannot be certain that this is the case in all classrooms.
20. Figure 9 displays teacher responses to one item that asks how often they expect their students to use technology in completing their class work or assignments. We chose this item because it fell in the middle of the difficulty range in our Rasch analyses when creating our overall measure of teacher technology use (see Appendix B for further details on methods).

21 The item being represented in Figure 10 asks whether their school is preparing students to be proficient in the use of technology. We chose this item because it best represents teachers' responses to all items in our "Teacher-reported Culture" measure (see Appendix B for further details on methods).

22 Hart, Allensworth, Lauen, and Gladden (2002).

23 These models add two teacher measures, "Teacher Use" and "Teacher-reported Culture" to the final student model presented in Chapter 2.

24 As can be seen in Table C.5 in Appendix C, at both the elementary and high school level, each of our two teacher measures individually helped explain school-by-school differences in student use, but to a lesser degree than the two combined. Also notable is that the variance explained is lower at the elementary level than at the high school level. This may be partially due to the large effect of selective enrollment schools for high school students.

Chapter 3

25 Coca and Allensworth (2007); Hart, Allensworth, Lauen, and Gladden (2002).

26 Coca and Allensworth (2007).

27 Because there is only one principal per school surveyed, we look at all principals' responses together rather than breaking them down by elementary and high school.

28 Coca and Allensworth (2007).

29 Hart, Allensworth, Lauen, and Gladden (2002).

30 Because our data do not link students into classrooms (or by teacher), we cannot conduct a 3-level model with students nested within teachers nested within schools.

Chapter 4

31 Lenhart, Purcell, Smith, and Zickuhr (2010).

32 Bebell, O'Dwyer, Russell, and Hoffman (2010); Lie (2010); Warschauer and Matuchniak (2010).

33 This is similar to a suggestion made by Hillarious and Milman (2012).

34 NGA and CCSSO (2010).

35 NCES, (2012).

36 Penuel (2006).

37 For example, Roschelle, Penuel, and Abrahamson (2004).

38 Hart, Allensworth, Lauen, and Gladden (2002).

39 For example, Anderson and Dexter (2005).

40 ISTE (2009).

41 For example, Anthony (2012) and Dexter (2011).

42 Hart, Allensworth, Lauen, and Gladden (2002).

Appendix B

43 If a student has multiple ninth-grade EXPLORE scores, we used the first one in our files.

ABOUT THE AUTHORS

STACY B. EHRLICH is a Senior Research Analyst at the CCSR. Along with studying technology use in Chicago Public Schools (CPS), she is studying YOUmedia, a digital media space for teens at the Chicago Public Library. She is also conducting research on the reasons for and the impacts of early chronic absenteeism in CPS. Prior work, at Education Development Center, Inc. (EDC), included conducting research responding to states' educational policy concerns, and a study on a preschool science professional development program. Ehrlich earned her BS in human development and family studies from the University of Wisconsin-Madison, and an MA and PhD in developmental psychology from the University of Chicago.

SUSAN E. SPORTE is Director for Research Operations at CCSR. Her current research focuses on teacher preparation and measuring effective teaching. She serves as the main point of contact with Chicago Public Schools regarding data sharing and research priorities; she also oversees CCSR's data archive. Prior to joining CCSR, she worked as a community college math instructor, field evaluator for a not-for-profit agency, and college administrator. Sporte received a BS in mathematics from Michigan State University, an MA in mathematics from the University of Illinois at Springfield, and an EdM and EdD in administration, planning, and social policy from the Harvard Graduate School of Education.

PENNY BENDER SEBRING is a Senior Research Associate at the University of Chicago and Founding Co-Director of CCSR. She is currently leading research on YOUmedia Chicago, and she is co-author of *Organizing Schools for Improvement: Lessons from Chicago* (University of Chicago Press, 2010). She graduated with a BA in Sociology from Grinnell College, where she is a life member of the Board of Trustees. She received a PhD in Education and Policy Studies from Northwestern University. Sebring serves on the Board of Directors for the Chicago Public Education Fund, and she is chair of the Policy Advisory Board of the School of Education and Social Policy at Northwestern University.

This report reflects the interpretation of the authors. Although CCSR's Steering Committee provided technical advice, no formal endorsement by these individuals, organizations, or the full Consortium should be assumed.

UCHICAGOCCSR

CONSORTIUM ON CHICAGO SCHOOL RESEARCH

Directors

ELAINE M. ALLENSWORTH
Interim Executive Director
Consortium on Chicago School Research

JENNY NAGAOKA
Deputy Director
Consortium on Chicago School Research

MELISSA RODERICK
Hermon Dunlap Smith Professor
School of Social Service Administration
University of Chicago

PENNY BENDER SEBRING
Founding Director
Consortium on Chicago School Research

Steering Committee

LILA LEFF
Co-Chair
Umoja Student Development Corporation

MATTHEW STAGNER
Co-Chair
Chapin Hall Center for Children

Institutional Members

CLARICE BERRY
Chicago Principals and Administrators Association

JENNIFER CHEATHAM
Chicago Public Schools

CHRISTOPHER KOCH
Illinois State Board of Education

KAREN G.J. LEWIS
Chicago Teachers Union

Individual Members

VERONICA ANDERSON
Communications Consultant

ANDREW BROY
Illinois Network of Charter Schools

AMIE GREER
Vaughn Occupational High School-CPS

RAQUEL FARMER-HINTON
University of Wisconsin, Milwaukee

REYNA HERNANDEZ
Illinois State Board of Education

TIMOTHY KNOWLES
Urban Education Institute

DENNIS LACEWELL
Urban Prep Charter Academy for Young Men

PETER MARTINEZ
University of Illinois at Chicago

RUANDA GARTH MCCULLOUGH
Loyola University

LISA SCRUGGS
Jenner and Block

LUIS R. SORIA
Ellen Mitchell Elementary School

BRIAN SPITTLE
DePaul University

KATHLEEN ST. LOUIS
Project Exploration

AMY TREADWELL
Chicago New Teacher Center

ARIE J. VAN DER PLOEG
American Institutes for Research

JOSIE YANGUAS
Illinois Resource Center

KIM ZALENT
Business and Professional People for the Public Interest

www.ingramcontent.com/pod-product-compliance
Lightning Source LLC
Chambersburg PA
CBHW060822090426
42738CB00002B/76